T

THE TROPICAL GARDEN

THE TROPICAL GARDEN

with 365 full-color illustrations

Text by William Warren

Photographs by Luca Invernizzi Tettoni

Thames and Hudson

© 1991 Thames and Hudson Ltd, London

First published in the United States in 1991 by Thames and Hudson Inc., 500 Fifth Avenue, New York, New York 10110

Library of Congress Catalog Card Number 91–65317

Printed and bound in Singapore

Contents

Introduction

Luxuriant, faintly mysterious, the tropical garden reflects many of man's oldest dreams with its never-ending growth and splashes of exotic colour.

Strelitzia
Reginae, *the Bird of Paradise flower; early drawings like this excited the European interest in tropical plants and led to both personal and official collections.* (Redouté les Liliacées, *v. 2, plate 78).*

FOR CENTURIES, LONG BEFORE it assumed any clearly defined shape, the alluring concept of a tropical garden was part of the European imagination. Eden was perhaps the earliest manifestation, that paradise of eternal bloom and fruitful abundance, whose loss seemed so painful to devout dreamers in the sands and snows of less hospitable climates; but there were doubtless other, more personal visions conjured up on dark winter nights, similar places where summer never ceased and nature yielded its marvels with little or no labour.

An element of reality entered such fantasies with the age of exploration, first through drawings and dried specimens brought back by adventurous botanists, later through some of the living plants, many of them every bit as bizarre as any of the vague imaginings. (The tropics hid no 'man-eating tree', as legend claimed, or at least none has been found; but in Borneo and the Philippines there were exceedingly odd pitcher plants that trapped and then slowly digested quite large insects.) Thanks to such revelations, painters could enhance their ideal gardens with increasingly accurate ferns and palms and exotic fruit trees – the banana often turned up as the tree of the knowledge of good and evil – even though the jungles in which they allegedly grew bore a remarkable resemblance to the neat, orderly arrangement of home.

The European fascination for tropical plants reached a peak during the 19th century, when scarcely any major capital, however frigid, lacked some sort of facility for displaying the latest botanic wonder to the public. Nowhere was this more evident than in England; moreover, odd though the suggestion may seem, it can also be argued that no country had a greater influence on the subsequent development of pleasure garden designs and their plant components far away in the actual tropics.

An artist's vision of paradise: 'The Garden of Eden' by Erastus F. Salisbury, c. 1865; greater knowledge of the tropics led to increased botanical accuracy in such paintings.

As their empire spread, it became possible for the English to travel in comparative safety to the rain forests of Borneo and Malaya, to the lush islands of the West Indies, to Central America, India, Burma, and the South Pacific – to the native habitats, that is, of just about every tropical plant. (To give some idea of this wealth, Malaya alone offered some 8,000 species.) Given their long-established passion for horticulture back home, not to mention a growing demand from wealthy plant collectors and such celebrated botanic centers as Kew, it was not surprising that many of these wanderers sought to bring back a few specimens for both pleasure and profit.

Also unsurprisingly, their early efforts more often than not ended in disaster. Live plants usually died during the long sea

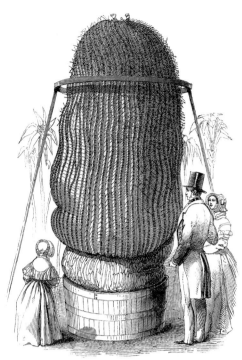

"MONSTER CACTUS," AT THE ROYAL BOTANIC GARDENS, KEW.

*F*ascinated *Victorians view a new exotic specimen at Kew (from* The Illustrated London News, *17 October 1846).*

*D*rawing of a *Wardian case for carrying plants and seeds from exotic places, from* N. Ward, Closed Cases for Plants *(British Library).*

voyages of the time, and seeds were not that much more successful, either having lost their viability by the time they arrived or, if they were successfully germinated, soon withering in the hostile climate.

The 'greenhouse' or 'conservatory' — two words that originated in the 17th century — was an early effort to overcome this problem. The Orangery at Kew, built in 1761, was at first heated by hot-air flues, later by hot water. Temperatures were difficult to control in such structures, however, and the extensive use of glass to increase the tropical atmosphere was for a long time curtailed by both a lack of good-quality sheet glass and a prohibitive tax.

A major breakthrough took place in 1827 when a London physician named Nathaniel Ward, by way of experiment, placed a caterpillar in a glass jar with a bit of mould and then stoppered the jar. He apparently forgot about it, and when he inspected the jar later he found that a small fern and a blade of grass were growing out of the mould, nurtured by moisture that had condensed on the inside.

There is no record of what happened to the caterpillar — presumably the object of the original experiment — but the plants flourished for four years and the discovery gave birth to the famous Wardian case which, in the words of Tyler Whittle in his delightful book *The Plant Hunters*, 'so revolutionized the transport of exotics that plant hunting up to 1834 might appropriately be called pre-Wardian, and the intensive collecting done afterward, post-Wardian.'

Ward produced a large-sized version of his jar, consisting of glass panes supported by hard, seasoned wood. One result of this was a rage for what were called terraria, little indoor gardens that became a familiar item of Victorian interior decoration. Another, far more important, was a dramatic improvement in the survival rate of plants moved from one part of the world to another. Thanks to the so-called Wardian cases (from which, incidentally, the doctor derived no profits), delicate tropical specimens arrived safely in England and elsewhere from distant places, there to be proudly installed in huge, glass-covered gardens that were also fortuitously entering a period of mass popularity around the same time.

The development of these glasshouses was an outgrowth of the repeal of Britain's Glass Tax in 1845, together with the rise of new industries producing quality glass at far lower cost than ever before. Literally thousands of such structures appeared in England

The great Palm House at Kew, built by Decimus Burton between 1844 and 1848 to display palms and other ornamental plants brought from the tropics (from The Illustrated London News, *7 August 1852).*

– 'Tropic Squares' they were called by the Poet Laureate of the day – ranging from tiny outhouses in suburban backyards to Decimus Burton's splendid Palm House at Kew, constructed between 1844 and 1848 and covering 24,200 square feet; and wealthy collectors vied to see who could amass the greatest number of exotic plants for their own increasingly grand private glasshouses.

The sixth Duke of Devonshire, for instance, sent one of his gardeners, a young man named John Gibson, to India in 1835 with the particular mission of bringing back an *Amherstia nobilis*, reputed to be the most beautiful flowering tree in the world with its masses of coral-coloured blossoms. Despite acute suffering from the heat, which somehow came as a surprise, Gibson got his *Amherstia*,

Joseph Paxton's
Great Conservatory at
Chatsworth, at its time the largest
glass-covered area in the world
(from the Devonshire Collection).

along with a collection of other tropical specimens that filled thirteen of the then-new Wardian cases, and then raced back to England on the fastest possible ship. Joseph Paxton, the Duke's head gardener, had constructed a special glasshouse to receive the tender plants and was at the port to meet Gibson and speed the cases to Chatsworth by a relay team of coaches.

Paxton became the most famous of all glasshouse designers. His Great Conservatory at Chatsworth, built between 1836 and 1840, was the largest glass-covered area in the world, wide enough for Queen Victoria to ride through in her carriage. Another similar glasshouse on the estate enabled the Duke to enjoy the first English flowering of the huge Brazilian water lily, given the name

Victoria Regia in honour of the Queen (the name was later changed to *Victoria Amazonica*). Kew also built a special house for the *Victoria*, designed by Richard Turner and completed in 1852, and so did almost every major botanical garden in Europe; the platter-like leaves became as much a part of the popular tropical-garden image as the elegant Traveller's Palm and the giant-leafed *Alocasia*, or 'Elephant's Ear'.

Both the Wardian case and the great Victorian glass-houses played prominent roles in the development of ornamental landscapes in the tropics as we know them today. Economic gardens had been important to hot-weather colonial possessions since the early days of empire, mainly for experiments with plants of potential commercial value. The one at St Vincent in the West Indies was established in 1764 (Captain William Bligh was headed there in the *Bounty* with a cargo of young breadfruit trees when the famous mutiny broke out), and others followed in Jamaica (1774), Calcutta (1786), Penang (1796), Ceylon (1821), and Singapore (1822). Wardian cases greatly facilitated the task of bringing new specimens to these centres, not only such future money-earners as rubber, coffee, oil palm, and spices but countless ornamentals as well. This accelerated the dispersal that would eventually bring exotic plants from the jungles of Central America to gardens in Singapore, from the South Seas to Trinidad, many of them quickly becoming so acclimatized that within a few generations they were regarded as almost native species.

The Great Conservatory at Chatsworth (top), where the sixth Duke of Devonshire kept his collection of tropical exotics.

A Victoria Regia flower, by J. F. Allen.

The Victoria Regia, (now Amazonica) water lily (bottom), in a glasshouse constructed especially for its cultivation by Joseph Paxton at Chatsworth.

To cite but a few common examples, the Bougainvillea, Allamanda, Plumeria, Poinsettia, Heliconia, Anthurium, Bromeliad, and Philodendron – now standard garden plants throughout the tropical world – all originated in Central and South America, and most were introduced elsewhere during the past century.

The influence of the glasshouses was more subtle but no less significant. To understand it, one must remember that the concept of a private garden planted purely for aesthetic purposes was generally alien to tropical countries. Many royal palaces and religious buildings, it is true, had gardens, though more often than not these were rather formal and symbolic, with the choice of plants and sometimes even their location being determined by a number of mystical factors. In the highly developed urban centres of ancient India, wealthier families also planted extensive pleasure parks of trees and shrubs with fragrant flowers (particularly those mentioned in poetry) as well as artificial lakes and pools, often with fountains.

But there was no such tradition of ornamental horticulture among the inhabitants of most hot-weather places. Around the average home there might be a few specimens chosen especially because of their scented flowers or because they were believed to bring good fortune; the greatest number of plants, however, were strictly utilitarian, grown for their fruits or medicinal properties rather than for the pleasure of viewing their flowers or foliage. Nor would much, if any, attention be paid to attractive landscape design in such gardens: early accounts by travellers in the tropics abound in enthusiastic descriptions of jungle scenery, but a reader will search in vain for one praising the tasteful arrangement of massed ornamental beds and contrasting lawns of well-trimmed grass around the homes of natives.

These features were largely European contributions to the tropical garden and many of them were based on memories of effects seen in those glass-covered wonderlands back in England, Holland, and France with their tastefully arranged collections of ferns and lacy palms, their imaginative use of meandering pathways and man-made water features, above all, perhaps, their fondness for beds of colourful shrubs, chosen for either their flowers or leaf patterns, a 19th-century garden fashion both inside the glasshouses and out.

Such 'tame jungles', as one writer has called them, were generally first seen in the great botanical gardens like Buitenzorg

('Free of Care') at Bogor, which served as the official residence of the Governors-General of the Dutch East Indies, and Singapore, in which, from its beginning, large areas were designed for pleasant evening strolls and Sunday-afternoon band concerts. They were later emulated on a smaller scale in private compounds, initially those of colonial officials and later spreading to the more Westernized local upper classes.

The development was slower in the rare tropical countries that escaped colonization, of which Thailand is the only example in Southeast Asia. M.R. Pimsai Amranand, whose *Gardening in Bangkok* is the standard work on the subject, writes that when she returned from many years of study in England, 'My first impression of gardens in Bangkok was of flat pieces of land with spindly fruit trees planted all along the fences, with herbs and flowers planted in ugly raised beds completely straight, looking vaguely like graves . . . The emphasis was on the plants with little thought of how a garden should look or of making a garden. The word "suan" in Thai and translated as "garden" conjures up in Thai minds a place that the English would call an orchard or market garden.'

Today, a mere twenty years after her book was first published, Bangkok abounds in fine examples of what is generally perceived as 'the tropical garden' – that is, an artful blend of exotic plants and basically European concepts of landscape design, in many cases far more spacious than the glasshouse arrangements of the past but not unlike them in general effect.

This sort of modern tropical garden belongs to no particular place or culture, if indeed it ever did. With the advent of air travel, the dispersal of ornamentals has accelerated at such a rate that new plants are constantly being introduced, getting acclimatized, and turning into standards within an amazingly short time. When the Bali Hyatt Hotel opened in 1973, for instance, hundreds of trees, shrubs, and ground covers were used in its extensive gardens, many brought from nearby Singapore but others from as far as Hawaii and South America; today most of these can be found all over Bali, not only in gardens but growing wild in the jungles. Of more than 100 specimens photographed for a book published in 1977 on tropical exotics found in Hawaiian gardens, only one was native to Hawaii and the great majority were fairly late introductions, some so recent that the authors were able to name the collectors who had brought them to the islands.

Given only the plant material to judge from, then, minus any revealing architectural features, it would be impossible to say whether most contemporary tropical gardens are located in Bali or Bangkok, Singapore or Miami, Honolulu or Kandy.

Moreover, the term 'tropical' can be misleading, particularly to a layman, suggesting a certain uniformity of conditions: constant heat, of course, plentiful rainfall, rich soil. In fact, conditions vary almost as much in the tropics as in temperate countries, not just from country to country but even within a single locale. Cibodas on Java is a tropical garden, but it is located at an elevation of nearly 2,000 metres and the weather is cool enough to support numerous temperate-zone plants as well. Thailand certainly qualifies as tropical in terms of temperature, but many parts of the country have almost no rain at all for nearly half the year and soil conditions are so diverse that a separate gardening book would be required for each region. Without leaving the residential suburbs of Honolulu, one can find an assortment of micro-climates ranging from wet to dry, from sea level to fairly high elevations, each quite different in the demands it makes on a horticulturist.

Given these differences, no work of the present sort, covering gardens in several parts of the tropical world, could hope to provide any very practical information on cultivation. Its purpose, rather, is to show some of the ways garden owners in the tropics have made creative use of their varied landscapes, climates, and plant material. Gardeners elsewhere might find useful inspiration through certain features – a pleasing pathway, an unusual fountain, an interesting combination of colours or leaf textures, even the plants themselves (many of which can be grown far from their tropical homelands) – or they might merely discover new images which which to adorn the ancient, ever-compelling dream of paradise.

A grove of Ficus trees spread their dramatic aerial roots along a road in Hawaii.

Religious and Royal Gardens

*A reclining Buddha image under a Bodhi tree (*Ficus religiosa*) near the old Thai capital of Ayutthaya.*

A pond in a Thai Buddhist temple at Petchburi serves an aesthetic as well as a practical function. The building on the right is a library, built over the water to protect manuscripts from white ants.

*T*he earliest gardens of the tropics were those planted in the compounds of religious complexes and around the palaces of local royalty. A simple desire for beautiful surroundings was seldom the sole motive in creating these landscapes. Symbolism and tradition were often equally important factors, not only in architectural and decorative features but also in the selection of plants to be included and their precise locations. Nevertheless, within their various cultures, such gardens helped set aesthetic standards which in sometimes subtle ways can be detected in many contemporary designs.

IT IS DIFFICULT, IF NOT IMPOSSIBLE, to accurately reproduce the original gardens of most tropical palaces and religious complexes. None has been preserved unchanged over the centuries: in some cases, the architectural concept remains but new plants have been introduced and entirely different (often European-inspired) landscape designs have been superimposed, while in others the buildings have vanished altogether and the only sources are vague descriptions in official chronicles. Yet there were certainly gardens, often quite beautiful ones, and they were undoubtedly the earliest to be planted in the tropics; moreover, even from the scant evidence at hand it is possible to make a few general comments on their design and components.

Not surprisingly, given the climate, water was an important element, in religious compounds as well as royal pleasure gardens. Hindu, Buddhist, and Chinese temples all incorporated ponds, pools, fountains, and often extensive artificial lakes in their landscapes, either for ritual bathing or merely decoration and a cooling effect. In many cases – the Hindu temples of Bali, for example – such water features displayed complex engineering skills, involving aqueducts and ornamental fountains, and formed an integral part of the architectural concept. In others, designs of pools reflected familiar emblems of the religion; a famous one at Anuradhapura, the ancient capital of Sri Lanka, is in

A Bodhi tree growing on one of the terraces of the Shwedagon Pagoda in Rangoon.

Stone figure used as a fountain at Goa Gajah, the 'Elephant Cave', an 11th-century religious site in Bali.

The Lotus Pool at Anuradhapura, ancient capital of Sri Lanka.

Tirta Empul, one of the most sacred places in Bali, dating from the 10th century; the spring from which the water comes is known as 'the Fountain of Immortality'. By regarding places of unusual beauty as holy and re-landscaping them in the form of gardens, the Balinese have succeeded in preserving the environment and creating what is possibly the most beautiful island on earth.

the shape of a huge lotus blossom, the petals serving as steps to the deepest part.

Symbolism played an important role in the choice of plants for such gardens, with special prominence given to trees and shrubs that had acquired some sort of spiritual significance. The most important of these throughout tropical Asia were various species of Ficus, particularly *Ficus religiosa*, the so-called Bodhi tree, under which the Buddha is believed to have attained enlightenment. Buddhists, however, are not alone in attributing mystical qualities to Ficus trees; perhaps because of their spectacular aerial roots, which often form strange, twisted patterns and mysterious grottos, they have long been seen as an obvious abode for supernatural powers and thus also venerated by Hindus as well as by countless animistic groups.

In temple gardens, both modern and ancient, a large Ficus is nearly always given a special enclosure of its own, with some sort of shrine or altar nearby where offerings can be made. The tree is carefully tended, specialists being called in when disease

23

strikes and the branches of an ageing specimen supported by poles to keep them from breaking; one at Anuradhapura is supposedly the oldest historical tree in the world, having been brought from India as a seedling in 288 BC and its life recorded ever since.

Of almost equal significance is *Nelumbo nucifera*, the lotus, which has acquired a wide-ranging collection of symbolic connotations, including fertility, prosperity, perfection, and the transitory nature of human existence. The lotus thrives in both tropical and temperate climates and is found in religious compounds from India to Japan, growing in lakes, moats, ornamental pools and large jars, as well as depicted in mural paintings, stone and wood carvings, ceramic designs, and architectural details.

24

Left: the poles around a venerable Bodhi tree at Wat Phra That Lampang Luang in northern Thailand are both offerings to the sacred tree and also supports to keep its branches from breaking.

Balinese offerings, collectively known as banten, *come in a vast variety of shapes, colours, and materials, as those shown on this and the facing page suggest. In many, symbolism plays a part in both the colour and the number of flowers used and also in the shape of the offering. The* banten *at the bottom of this page, called* jejaitan, *are made of cut, plaited, and pinned palm leaves.*

*P*lants figure
prominently in classical Balinese
paintings, as in these from the
Kerta Gosa Hall of Justice, part
of the palace at Klungkung.

A more decorative tree than the Ficus is the Plumeria, popularly called Frangipani, a native of tropical America which has been cultivated in Asia for at least two centuries; in India it is sometimes known as the 'Temple tree' and is planted in Muslim cemeteries as well as Buddhist monastery gardens. Perhaps because of these associations, the tree was once considered unsuitable for private gardens in some places, though this aversion does not seem to have been very strong. (In Thailand, it was based more on linguistic than religious grounds; the local name, *lamtom*, sounds like *ra-tom*, the Thai word for 'sorrow', and thus the tree was thought to bring unhappiness.)

Saracas, natives of Southeast Asia from Malaysia to India, were used in many religious gardens for shade and for the beauty of their displays of yellow, orange, or red flowers, and so were various species of Brownea, which have large red or pink flower heads. A number of scented shrubs and creepers – Jasmine, for instance, and *Michelia alba* – were also popular, partly because of their fragrance and partly because they provided a ready source of flowers for the garlands presented in large quantities as offerings.

Water features were a prominent part of royal compounds as well. The Taman Sari, also known as the 'Water Castle' and used for recreation by the Sultans of Yogyakarta in Java, was an

The Kraton (Royal Palace) of Yogyakarta; such open pavilions allowed the gardens and pools to become an integral part of palace life.

The bathing pools at Tirtagangga – literally, 'Ganges Water' – part of a former palace in Bali and now popular with local children (opposite).

ingenious aquatic pleasure palace, surrounded by a broad moat and containing innumerable canals, conduits, ponds, and intimate private bathing pools. At Klungkung on the island of Bali, the Puri Smarapura ('Palace of the God of Love') had a graceful pavilion with painted ceilings in the centre of a lake, fed by water that spurted from the mouths of stone animals, while at Tirtagangga – literally, though not accurately, 'Ganges Water' – there is an extensive network of once-royal ponds and fountains, now a popular bathing spot for local children.

Plants, too, were often similar, with the notable exception of *Ficus religiosa*. Flowering trees and shrubs with scented flowers were popular, especially those frequently mentioned in poetry like *Saraca indica*, *Michelia alba*, and Jasmine, and many gardens also contained specimens used in cooking, traditional medicines, and making the complex floral offerings that were often a speciality of palace women. Symbolism, however, still played a significant role: at the Kraton (Royal Palace) of Yogyakarta, the choice and exact siting of plants was determined by a complex (and, to an outsider, somewhat obscure) pattern based

*P*art of the
*Siwalai Garden in Bangkok's
Grand Palace; Ixora are among
the clipped shrubs that line the
pathways of this private garden,
reserved for the royal family.*

on their local names, which in turn suggested such concepts as 'hopeful', 'youth', and 'mutual understanding'.

More subject to changing fashions than religious compounds, palace landscapes were the first to respond to Western innovations and today few, if any, exist in their original form. A notable example is the Siwalai Garden of Bangkok's Grand Palace,

intended as a recreation area for the sizeable population of royal wives and children who lived in an adjacent walled section which even today, long after the last resident has departed, is closed to most outsiders. The palace was constructed between 1782 and 1785 as a replica of one in the former capital of Ayutthaya, and both it and the garden were extensively altered over the next century or so.

29

Under the Bangkok dynasty's second king, for example, the Siwalai Garden was dominated by a large lake containing several islands; on these there were Chinese-style pavilions and a small theatre where classical Thai dramas were performed. The third king, a pious Buddhist, disapproved of such frivolity and dismantled most of the garden, though retaining some of the Chinese statuary which adorned it. King Rama IV partially restored the area and added a personal chapel in traditional Thai style faced with grey marble.

The garden that remains today was essentially laid out in the fifth reign — a rectangular expanse flanked at one end by the Western-style Baromphiman Mansion and at the other by a classic Thai structure built in 1879 to house statues of past kings, with King Rama IV's chapel in the middle. Numerous Plumeria trees are planted in the lawns, and pathways are lined with fragrant shrubs, often clipped in the geometric shapes popular in both royal and religious Thai gardens. Chinese influence, strong during much of the 19th century, is evident in stone figures used as decorations and in two moon gates leading through one wall into the former women's quarter.

Elsewhere in Bangkok is another royal garden surrounding the all-teakwood Vimarn Mek Palace, built in 1900 by King Rama V and restored by Her Majesty Queen Sirikit in 1982 as part of the dynasty's bicentennial celebration. The present planting is a blend of original trees and newer ornamentals – mostly shrubs and annuals – added during the restoration. The tallest trees in the compound belong to the Dipterocarpus family, indigenous to Thailand and a source of much-valued hard wood for furniture. *Vatica scortechini* and *Ochrocarpus siamensis*, also native trees, are planted close to the palace; both have small but fragrant flowers and the latter is also used in traditional Thai medicine. A number of fruit trees like Mango, Tamarind, Custard Apple, and Jackfruit further reflect the old Thai philosophy that even royal landscapes should be practical as well as aesthetically appealing.

Part of the garden at Vimarn Mek Palace; most of this area was re-landscaped during restoration of the palace in 1982.

*A European
statue in a covered pavilion at the
entrance to Vimarn Mek.*

*Shrubs selected
for their flowers and colourful
foliage, near one of the auxiliary
buildings in the palace gardens.*

Botanical Gardens

A massed display of Begonias and other ornamental plants in a glasshouse at Sri Lanka's famous Peradeniya Botanical Garden.

*O*rnamentals from various parts of the world have been introduced into a rich natural environment at the Lyon Arboretum in Hawaii.

*O*riginally created as centres of scientific research where potential commercial crops could be tested, the great tropical botanical gardens also played a major role in the dispersal of ornamental plants throughout the world and, in some cases, have produced hybrids that later became popular standards. Moreover, most were designed to provide aesthetic pleasure as well as to serve as a showcase for collections, and their often European landscape features – artificial lakes and sweeping lawns, atmospheric pathways and massed beds of exotic specimens – provided a powerful inspiration to private gardeners.

A memorial built by Thomas Stamford Raffles to his wife Olivia, who died at Bogor during Raffles' brief tenure as Governor of Java.

THE FIRST BOTANICAL GARDEN in the tropics was Pamplemousses, established on the Indian Ocean island of Mauritius in 1735. Over the next century, numerous others followed as European countries acquired more and more colonial possessions, eventually forming a horticultural network that stretched around the world from the West Indies to Southeast Asia.

Nearly all such gardens were originally economic, places for testing various new crops that might be grown commercially, and in this effort they were dramatically successful; Pamplemousses, for example, helped develop the vital sugar industry of Mauritius, and the Singapore Botanical Garden was responsible for introducing rubber to Malaya. At the same time, they also acclimatized countless ornamental specimens brought from distant places, and since most such gardens served a recreational as well as a scientific purpose they exerted a powerful influence on the development of modern tropical garden designs.

One of the oldest and most celebrated of Asia's botanical gardens is the Kebun Raya at Bogor in Java. Though located at an altitude of only 260 metres on the slope of Mount Salak, Bogor enjoys much cooler weather than the capital of Jakarta, some 54 kilometres to the north, and this is what led the Dutch Governor-General Baron Gustaaf von Imhoff to build a summer house there in 1744. He called it Buitenzorg ('Free of Care'), and it continued to be known by this name for the remaining two centuries of Dutch rule, during which the Baron's house was replaced by a much

An avenue of Canarium trees at the Kebun Raya, festooned with assorted creepers and epiphytic plants; one 19th-century visitor called this 'the finest avenue of trees in the world'.

37

grander, white-columned structure that from 1870 to 1942 served as the residence of Governors-General of the Dutch East Indies.

It was not the Dutch, however, who originally conceived the idea of planting a botanical garden around Buitenzorg. As one of the complex international results of the Napoleonic Wars, the British briefly occupied Java and from 1811 to 1816 their representative was Thomas Stamford Raffles, later to achieve fame as the founder of Singapore. A keen amateur botanist, Raffles was also a strong believer in the value of 'economic gardens' and saw that Bogor was an ideal site for one with its rich volcanic soil and plentiful rainfall. He is sometimes also credited with laying out the design of the Kebun Raya, but this was in fact done by Professor C.G.L. Reinwardt and two assistants from Kew, in England; the garden was officially opened in 1817, the year after Raffles left.

Tree ferns and Birds' Nest Ferns thrive in the cool air of Cibodas, a high-elevation extension of the Kebun Raya garden.

*E*piphytes grow
on the gnarled trunks of century-
old trees at Bogor.

Victoria
Amazonica *water lilies in a pond*
at the Kebun Raya garden.

*T*ree ferns
(Cyathea) *in one of the misty
valleys at Cibodas, a garden with
unusually high rainfall at an
elevation of nearly 2,000 metres.*

When the Dutch returned, they so improved and expanded the Kebun Raya that by the end of the century it was known as one of the world's foremost tropical plant collections. Important research was done on such commercial crops as tea, cassava, tobacco, oil palm, and chichona (quinine), all of which contributed to Indonesia's wealth. In addition, surrounding the palace as it did, the garden became equally famous as an imaginatively landscaped pleasure park for members of the colonial élite who maintained homes nearby.

Particularly dramatic was its main drive lined with towering Canarium trees – 'the finest avenue of trees in the world', one visitor called it – each trunk covered with a tangled mass of staghorn and birds' nest ferns, Philodendrons (one of the many ornamentals introduced to Southeast Asia at Bogor), and epiphytic orchids, among them the giant Grammatophyllum, which has as many as 3,000 flowers at one blooming. Sweeping lawns were laid out, too, both around the palace and elsewhere in the garden, and the massed beds then so popular in Europe were planted with a wide assortment of exotic specimens to provide both flowers and colourful foliage.

The Kebun Raya today contains an estimated 15,000 species of trees and plants, as well as over 5,000 orchid varieties. One part of the 200-acre site has been left in its original rain-forest condition, while others are devoted to special collections, such as

An English-style landscape in the Penang Botanical Garden.

Flower of a Cycad in Honolulu's Foster Botanical Garden (opposite top).

Amherstia nobilis, regarded by many as the most beautiful flowering tree (centre).

Flowers of the Cannonball tree (bottom).

Seeds growing out of the trunk of the so-called Cannonball Tree (far left).

ferns, cacti, medicinal plants, palms, and bamboos. The best-maintained areas are those surrounding the palace, where tame deer (originally introduced by the Dutch as a source of venison) graze the lawns, and an extensive recreational section along both sides of Queen Astrid Avenue, where there are beds of multi-coloured Cannas and such ornamental trees as *Amherstia nobilis*, a native of Burma often called the most beautiful flowering tree in the world.

Above Bogor, at an elevation of nearly 2,000 metres, is Cibodas, an extension of the Kebun Raya established by the Dutch in 1889 for experiments with specimens that prefer cooler weather. This is decidedly European in design and atmosphere, with vast sloping lawns and numerous trees and shrubs more associated with temperate zones than with the tropics, collected from as far as South Africa and Australia. Thanks to an exceptionally high rainfall, Cibodas is rich in ferns and among its more striking features are valleys filled with lofty Tree Ferns and numerous smaller varieties.

43

Houses of garden caretakers at Pamplemousses.

A lily pond at Pamplemousses, the first botanical garden established in the tropics.

At the pioneering Pamplemousses, what had begun mainly as a search for plants that might benefit colonial treasuries led eventually to the creation of a beautiful landscape; and this process was repeated elsewhere in the tropical world.

Sri Lanka also offered perfect conditions for a botanical garden. The idea was first raised by Sir Joseph Banks, Director of Kew, when the British took over the island in the early 19th century and the first efforts were made near Colombo. In 1821, however, the garden was moved to the royal capital of Kandy and there, known as Peradeniya, it became one of the showplaces of the East, renowned not only for its success with economic crops (it helped develop the Assam tea that is today Sri Lanka's principal export) but also for the beauty of its ornamental lawns and tree-lined walkways. (Over the objections of some of his associates, Lord Louis Mountbatten located his wartime headquarters in the gardens, calling it 'probably the most beautiful place in the world and a delightful place in which to work'.)

Part of the large collection of palms planted at Pamplemousses.

Singapore, like Bogor, owes its famous garden to Thomas Stamford Raffles, who planted a park of nutmeg, clove, and ornamental shrubs on Government Hill soon after his arrival in 1819. This first effort later foundered, but in 1859 a new, more spacious garden, designed principally for pleasure, was started by a private group called the Agri-Horticultural Society in the Tanglin District. Scenic roads and pathways were laid out, an artificial lake was excavated, and on a slight elevation, terraced and planted with flower beds, a regimental band began giving Sunday-afternoon concerts. Eventually, the Society's debts exceeded its income; in 1875 the garden was turned over to the government and finally became the botanical research centre Raffles had envisaged.

The Orchid Enclosure at the Singapore Botanical Garden (also shown opposite, below right).

*A*rundina, one of the staples of Singapore's cut-flower trade.

*D*endrobium, 'Madame Pompadour', now exported in large quantities.

*V*anda hybrid; to this species belongs Vanda Miss Joachim, a natural hybrid which is Singapore's national flower.

*P*aphiopedilum, one of the many ground orchids.

*T*he Orchid Enclosure at the Singapore Botanical Garden.

Opposite: vines and other ornamental creepers are grown over trellises around this formal courtyard at the Singapore Botanical Garden.

The Bandstand, one of the oldest landmarks in the Singapore garden.

A gazebo at the entrance to the garden's jungle, where mostly indigenous plants grow.

Its most celebrated commercial achievement was the introduction of rubber as a viable crop in Malaya, credit for which largely goes to a single-minded Director named Henry Nicholas Ridley, who discovered an innovative way of tapping the trees and earned the sobriquet of 'Mad Ridley' because of his fervent campaign to persuade planters to try *Hevea brasiliensis* instead of coffee. (The specimens he worked with were descendants of only eleven seedlings which reached Singapore in Wardian cases in 1877, having been germinated at Kew from Brazilian seeds.)

Cordylines,
known in Hawaii as Ti plants,
are collected in this part of the
Lyon Arboretum, where their
varied foliage provides a
dramatic splash of colour. The
leaves are exported in
considerable quantities for use in
flower arrangements.

Overleaf
(p. 52–53): part of the garden at
the Lyon Arboretum; the
variegated leaves on the right
belong to a dwarf species of Ficus.

50

While Ridley and others were changing the economy of the region, however, the Singapore garden remained the recreational centre planned by its founders, and countless new ornamental trees and shrubs, as well as orchid hybrids, were introduced there. It continued to function even during the Japanese occupation – two English botanists were allowed to stay out of prison camp to go on with their work – and, since the colony's independence, has been responsible not only for maintaining the original 84-acre site but also for implementing former Prime Minister Lee Kuan Yew's ambitious scheme to transform Singapore into a 'Garden City' with imaginative street plantings and public parks.

Another garden established by the British in the area was on the island of Penang in Malaya. Known as the Waterfall Gardens, this was planted in 1884, and while it never achieved the renown of Singapore as a centre of research it continues to be a popular recreational park.

Hawaii, America's tropical possession, also acquired a number of noted plant collections. As one botanist has written, 'every flower and plant we see in Hawaii is a traveller or the descendant of a traveller', since the islands originally rose from the sea as boiling masses of lava (a process that still continues) and whatever grows on them had to be brought in by one means or another. The earliest human settlers came from Polynesia, bringing such practical plants as the coconut, breadfruit, bamboo, and banana. Ornamentals arrived later, the great majority brought from all over the tropical world by local gardeners.

Reflecting this tradition of individual collecting, a number of Hawaii's best botanical gardens today began as private estates and retain many of their original landscape features. The Foster Botanic Garden, for example, now in downtown Honolulu, was started by a German doctor in the mid-19th century. He sold the property to Captain and Mrs Thomas Foster in 1867 and it was bequeathed to the city in 1930. Today, covering 20 acres, it is part of the Honolulu Botanic Gardens, which includes two other collections on the island of Oahu as well.

For 27 years, the director of the Foster Garden was Dr Harold Lyon, a noted orchid specialist who is also credited with introducing more than 10,000 ornamental trees and plants to Hawaii. The Lyon Arboretum at Manoa, now under the University of Hawaii, is a living monument to his horticultural achievements and contains an impressive collection of exotics in a setting that

encompasses dense, jungled valleys, exposed areas, and a variety of elevations. Though roughly divided into areas that highlight certain species – Cordylines, Gingers, Heliconias, Bromeliads, Aroids, ferns and the like – the Arboretum has been imaginatively landscaped to demonstrate the use of such plants for ornamental purposes.

A variety of Costus, native to Central and South America.

54

Bromeliads in flower at the Lyon Arboretum.

A jungle-like pathway at the Lyon Arboretum, where various ornamentals are grown along with the original forest cover; a Medinilla magnifica *blooms on the upper right, while below is a planting of* Impatiens.

Colonial Style

A house in Goa with a Mediterranean flavour, enhanced by a bright Bougainvillea; the window panes are made of seashells.

An old house from the colonial period on Mount Faber in Singapore, its spacious, park-like garden shaded by large trees.

*B*oth *urban areas and private gardens planted by Europeans who settled in various colonial possessions drew their inspirations from the remembered landscapes of home, particularly in the use of neatly clipped lawns and tree-lined drives. Even fast-growing, often unruly tropical shrubs and creepers achieved a sense of visual order when arranged in familiar beds and herbaceous borders. The influence of these arrangements on contemporary gardens was considerable and extended to a number of hot-weather countries – Thailand, for example – which had never undergone the colonial experience.*

EARLY EUROPEANS WHO CAME to the tropics had conflicting emotions about their environment. The more romantic were entranced by the splendid luxuriance that surrounded them and responded like Isabella Bird, who travelled through Malaya in 1883: 'Vegetation rich, profuse, endless, rapid, smothering, in all shades of vivid green, from the pea-green of spring and the dark velvety green of endless summer to the yellow-green of the plumage of the palm.' Others, probably the majority of those who actually took up residence in such places, found it vaguely threatening: undisciplined and somehow suggestive of a moral laxity. They wanted a more controlled landscape, in part to conjure up nostalgic memories of home but also symbolically to repel the riotous jungle (and possibly riotous natives) that loomed on all sides.

And so, for the most part, they tried to reproduce Dutch cities in Java, British ones in Burma, Malaya, and the West Indies, French ones in Indo-China, Spanish ones in the Philippines. 'On each side of these Canals', wrote a visitor to Batavia (now Jakarta) in 1817, 'are planted Rows of fine Trees, that are always green, which, with the Beauty and Regularity of the Buildings, make the Streets look very agreeable; so that I think this City (for the bigness) one of the neatest and most beautiful in the whole World.' Other travellers admired similar evidence of orderly rule in Singapore, Rangoon, Saigon, and Manila and deplored the lack of it in non-colonial capitals like Bangkok, which did not acquire its first proper, Western-style street until the mid-19th century (and then only because foreign residents complained to the king that their health was suffering for lack of a place to take an evening carriage ride).

As Victor Savage comments in *Western Expressions of Nature and Landscape in Southeast Asia*, 'Such cities showed how Western taste had impregnated itself on the landscape. Here was a landscape neither natural nor indigenous, but fashioned according to the dictates of Western culture, technology, and aesthetic taste

Veranda of the Presidential Palace at Bogor, overlooking the botanical gardens; the residence was built by the Dutch in the latter part of the 19th century.

... The grid street patterns, canals, avenues and alleys, gardens, the geometrical flower beds and generally the spatial system of the Southeast Asian colonial cities were not only beautiful to many Western travellers, they were also emblems of security and comfort, and signs of dignified culture and civilization.'

What was true of the cities was equally true of the private gardens planted around the spacious bungalows and Victorian mansions of early settlers. The pride of most was its lawn, that ultimate reflection of horticultural order, laboriously weeded and clipped by native gardeners – small armies of them in the case of the really great lawns like those surrounding the residences of higher government officials. Reproduced, too, were the neat flower beds and herbaceous borders of home, also kept sternly under control through constant care. In many places Westerners tried to increase the illusion through imported seeds and bulbs. 'Great efforts were made to grow English flowers,' a former memsahib was

Originally introduced as a source of venison by the Dutch, deer still graze the lawns of the Presidential Palace at Bogor in Indonesia.

Opposite: views of the garden of the Presidential Palace at Bogor, which the Dutch called Buitenzorg, 'Free of Care'. The statues were added by President Sukarno.

Victoria Amazonica in the reflecting lake at the entrance to the Presidential Palace.

60

quoted as saying in *Plain Tales from the Raj*, 'which generally looked rather sickly in the Indian climate. We could have had the most marvellous gardens with orchids and all sorts of things, but no, they must be English flowers.' Later, as the choice of tropical specimens was increased through the work of botanical gardens, more adventurous plantings appeared that achieved familar effects with quite different materials and to more lasting effect.

If relatively few of these colonial gardens achieved real distinction, the main reason was perhaps that, more often than not,

Shortage of labour was never a problem in the maintenance of European features in large colonial gardens; here a team of workers is shown rolling a lawn at the Gymkhana Club in Bombay.

A summer palace in the cool highlands of Java, near Cipanas; built by the Dutch around 1750, it was also a favourite retreat for Indonesia's President Sukarno.

the houses belonged to the government or to business firms and the occupants changed regularly through transfer and retirement; whereas one might make serious efforts at planting an imaginative landscape, his successor might consider the continual upkeep too burdensome and prefer to settle for just a lawn, some shade trees, and perhaps a few beds of cheerfully bright Cannas and Hibiscus to offset the prevalent, eternal green.

A house from the colonial period in Penang; the flowers are Delonix regia.

A mansion at Chandor in Goa, now a museum.

A Chinese mansion in Phuket, Thailand; Caladiums *grow in the foreground.*

*O*pposite: *an old mansion at Vagator, a small town on the sea in Goa; the bright colours of the house echo those of the Bougainvillea and shrubs in the garden.*

*T*he former *House of Justice in Jakarta, completed in 1870; it now serves as the Museum of Fine Arts.*

There were important exceptions, however, particularly the gardens of the grander official residences like Buitenzorg in Bogor, where the Governors-General of the Dutch East Indies lived. Aside from a need to display its symbolic status, Buitenzorg could draw upon the immense resources of the adjacent botanical garden, not only for a ready supply of new and interesting plants but also for experienced landscape designers who laid out an overall plan that is still impressive a century later. Drives were lined with flowering trees from throughout the tropical world and two artificial lakes were excavated – the one in front rather formal and Western, reflecting the elegant white-columned residence and planted with the huge Brazilian *Victoria Amazonica* water lilies

Opposite: the Istana at Kuching in Sarawak; this was the residence of the 'White Rajahs', members of the Brooke family, who ruled over Sarawak for a century.

Bignonia ignea, the 'Flaming Trumpet Vine', blooms in the garden of an old bungalow in Chiang Mai, Thailand.

that were all the rage in 19th-century Europe, and the one behind more irregular and natural, with a densely jungled island that served as a bird sanctuary.

The blend of apparently wild and meticulously maintained areas that one sees at the Bogor palace today was a reflection of the European movement away from rigidly formal plantings towards those that more closely approximated the random arrangements of nature. Tropical countries, of course, provided ideal opportunities for creating such landscapes, for nothing could be wilder looking than a patch of jungle, real or simulated, with its twisting vines and lush ferns, especially when it was contrasted with a trim lawn; and the best of the colonial gardens, both private and public, achieved this effect. In doing so, they forever altered local aesthetic concepts and led directly to the gardens of today.

The Contemporary Tropical Garden

A Japanese-style garden using tropical plants on the University of Hawaii campus, sheltered by large Rain Trees.

A private garden near Cibodas, in the highlands of Java, where Tree Ferns grow along with temperate-zone conifers.

*A*t its best, the contemporary tropical garden is an artful blend of contrasting effects: of wild-looking areas and others meticulously maintained, of sun and shade, of artificial and natural features. While it might emulate familiar temperate-garden features – the well-trimmed lawn, the clipped hedge, the mixed bed – it cannot aspire to a slowly maturing but essentially unchanging design. It must be planned for continual growth and constantly altering vistas, thus presenting a challenge to gardeners while also offering the boon of seeing their dreams realized within the span of a very few years.

The Mandai Gardens

JOHN AND AMY EDE have played an active role in Singapore gardening circles for more than forty years, introducing many plants to the island through their Mandai Gardens and also working with the Singapore Gardening Society, of which John Ede served as president for fourteen years.

Though the Mandai Gardens is primarily a commercial concern, specializing in orchids for export, one part has been landscaped to show how tropical plants can be employed in a garden. This consists of several areas both open and shady, with ponds, streams, and walkways along which ornamentals from all over the world can be seen. Heliconias, mainly from Central America, have been a particular interest of the Edes and they now have several dozen varieties ranging from dwarfs to gigantic stands several metres tall. These, together with such Alpinias as the so-called Red Ginger and a variety with bright yellow and green striped leaves, do well in Singapore's damp climate, where prolonged dry spells are rare.

The Mandai Gardens are also noted for their Mussaenda, especially a pink-flowering variety from the Philippines, as well as numerous unusual Dracaena, Calathea, and Cordylines, all of which bring year-round colour to a tropical garden with their splendidly patterned leaves.

Densely planted beds are separated by well-trimmed lawns to create a sense of size in what is actually a relatively small area. On the right, Mussaenda, a native of the Philippines, provides an almost continual show of flowers against a background of Chrysalidocarpus palms.

Overleaf (pp. 72–73): dominating one part of the garden is a showy Traveler's Palm (Ravenala madagascariensis), actually a member of the banana family. Elsewhere varied leaf texture and color is provided by ferns, Dracaenas, Dieffenbachia, Gingers, and other exotics.

71

The colourful bracts of a Red Ginger (Alpinia purpurata) stand out against a clump of Bamboo with variegated leaves.

On the left along a stream grows Cyperus alternifolius, the 'Umbrella Plant', while on the right is a variegated

dwarf Pandanus, *which makes a useful ground cover. In the background can be seen* Heliconia rostrata, *with pendant bracts.*

The bed on the right is accented by a tall stand of Dracaena fragrans *'Victoriae', which displays its colours best in* full sunlight; the mass planting to the left is composed of Heliconias and Gingers.

75

A Garden on Phuket

PHUKET IS A LARGE ISLAND in the Andaman Sea off Thailand's southern coast, featuring a number of spectacular beaches along its western shore as well as a few areas where the original dense rain-forest cover has been retained. Rich in tin deposits, as well as rubber and coconut plantations, it enjoyed a reputation as one of the country's most prosperous provinces long before its recent emergence as a major tourist destination brought a proliferation of hotels and other resort facilities.

The property John and Pannee Ault acquired on Patong Beach in 1982 consisted of some 12 acres of disused rubber plantation and secondary forest, running along both sides of a stream that flowed all year from a mountain behind. As gardeners, they were attracted by the reliable water supply – a rarity on Phuket – plus the varied topography and the fact that the site was protected from the monsoon winds that can severely damage more exposed ornamental plants near the sea. With a team of local labourers they selectively cleared part of the property, though leaving larger trees and some handsome sugar palms, created a series of terraces leading up to the house they built, and channelled the stream to form six ponds of varying sizes. A larger part was left more or less as it was, with indigenous plants and trees, though pathways were cut through the forest and bridges built over the meandering stream.

The result is a remarkable tropical garden in which landscaped areas merge with the wild ones and the eye is constantly surprised by unexpected vistas. The Aults collected plants not only from varied parts of Thailand but also from Malaysia, Hawaii, and Australia, among other places; the garden, for example, contains more than twenty varieties of Hibiscus, as well as numerous palms,

A Thai spirit house stands in the shade of a Cashew Nut Tree; the red bracts are those of Alpinia purpurata, *or Red Ginger, while the variegated leaves below are* Ophiopogon. *Little houses like this, always raised on a post, are believed to shelter the guardian spirits of a compound in Thailand.*

76

including a rare one (*Karedoxa dolphin*) with silvery leaves, which is now found only in the jungles of Phuket. The smooth, sweeping lawn that sets off the massed plantings and ponds to striking effect is in fact the native wild grass that was on the original site, kept trimmed until it formed a solid cover.

One of the ponds has been devoted to day-blooming water lilies and pink lotus, while another is given over exclusively to white lotus. Beds in and around the sunny lawn are planted with various kinds of Heliconia, both double and single Hibiscus, pink and white Mussaendas, Red Ginger (*Alpinia purpurata*), Ixora, and assorted palms, while flowering trees include Lagerstroemia, Flame of the Forest (Delonix), and Jacaranda. Shadier areas contain Spathiphyllums, Cordylines, Dieffenbachias, Costus, Dracaenas, ferns and Philodendrons. Though some ornamentals have

View from the upper level over the terraces leading down to the front of the property; the sea can be glimpsed through the coconut palms in the background. Most of the trees were on the site originally.

Karedoxa dolphin, a now rare palm native to Phuket which has leaves that are silvery on the bottom side; the Aults planted many of these in the jungle part of their garden.

79

been introduced into the jungle part of the garden, the pathways
are dominated by native Costus, ferns (including a creeping variety
with iridescent blue-green leaves), towering clumps of Pandanus,
wild bananas, and Ficus trees with dramatic roots.

Shortly after the photographs for this book were taken,
the Ault garden was sold. It is to be hoped that the new owners will
continue their horticultural work as well as their preservation of
Phuket's natural landscape.

*Near the front
entrance to the house, a large
Ixora provides a reliable splash of
colour with its clusters of scarlet
flowers, while a dwarf variety of
the same plant serves as a clipped*

*hedge; a Beaumontia grows over
the veranda.*

*Ponds formed by
diverting the stream that flows
through the garden are planted*

*with assorted water lilies; a few
clipped shrubs offer an interesting
contrast to what is otherwise an
informal planting against the
jungle backdrop.*

A small area on one side of the Moir house, visible through a large picture window, has been planted with Bromeliads in a range of subtle colours. Such plants are popular with gardeners in Hawaii for their foliage as well as for their occasional, spectacular displays of flowers.

taken, a spectacular display of showy pink blooms was also provided by a large *Medinilla magnifica*, a native of the Philippines that flowers for about two months in Hawaii. From the drawing room, a picture window divided into sections that give it the appearance of a Japanese screen looks out on more Bromeliads, the colours of which are reflected in cushions chosen for the couch. Behind the house, a shady brick terrace serves as an ideal growing environment for varied ferns, mosses, and epiphytic plants, while a more exposed area below contains an assortment of Gingers and Heliconias, many of which Mrs Moir employs in her flower arrangements.

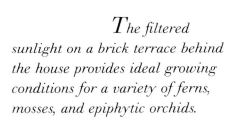

The filtered sunlight on a brick terrace behind the house provides ideal growing conditions for a variety of ferns, mosses, and epiphytic orchids.

Pink and white Phalaenopsis orchids cascade over potted Begonias in a conservatory attached to the house.

Shangri-La Hotel

A distinctive artificial waterfall spills into a pool in one part of the interior hotel garden. Palms, ferns, climbing Philodendrons, Spathiphyllum, and other carefully sited ornamentals increase the jungle-like atmosphere of the setting.

EVEN IN A CITY NOTED FOR its imaginative public plantings, Singapore's Shangri-La Hotel has gained exceptional renown for its garden, which in turn has exerted an influence on a number of others throughout the region today.

Designed by the American firm of Bell, Collins and Associates, the Shangri-La garden is an integral part of the hotel structure, extending even up its sides through dramatic masses of Bougainvillea hanging from balconies off the rooms – perhaps the hotel's most distinctive feature – and into open-access corridors and the lobby and restaurant areas as well. One courtyard on an upper level of the ground floor has been turned into a water garden, densely planted with ground covers, palms, ferns, and other tropical exotics, and a cascade that falls into another luxuriant garden near the coffee shop below.

Birds' Nest Ferns (Asplenium nidus), Crinum lilies, wild ferns, and other moisture-loving plants enhance the effect of an artificial stream.

The exterior garden is divided into various sections, some, like those near the swimming pool, left relatively open with lawns and scattered coconut palms and flowering trees, and others offering a more jungle-like atmosphere with huge bamboos that were already growing on the site, Red Gingers, Heliconias, Philodendrons, and beds of white-flowering Spathiphyllum.

Reminiscent of hotel plantings in Hawaii and elsewhere in tropical America, where the same designers have worked extensively, the Shangri-La garden was one of the first to employ the concepts in Southeast Asia. Its success has led to an enhanced awareness of how greatly such integrated garden features can add beauty to an otherwise utilitarian architecture, increasingly apparent not only in many of the newer hotels but also in airports, offices, and other public buildings.

An open outside corridor overlooks a dense planting of low ornamentals interspersed with Plumerias and toddy palms.

Spathiphyllum, Tree Ferns, Birds' Nest Ferns, Cordylines, and varied palms are planted in a sloping atrium garden leading down to the coffee shop.

Opposite: one of the Shangri-La's most distinctive features is its use of massed Bougainvillea in planter boxes, not only providing a dramatic display of colour but also softening the architecture and creating the effect of an almost continuous garden, vertical as well as horizontal.

In the outside gardens, beds of plants chosen for their contrasting leaf colours as well as flowers form islands in the lawns.

A view of the hotel's planter boxes; most of the exterior palms and trees were on the site when the hotel was built.

103

Batujimbar Gardens, Sanur Beach, Bali

MUCH OF BALI'S LEGENDARY ALLURE for Western romantics can be said to have originated at Sanur, not far from the capital of Denpasar, for it was here that some of the earliest foreign enthusiasts built bungalows on the scenic beach and produced their influential books, films, and photographs. These included Katharane Edson Mershon, a dancer-ethnologist who together with painter Walter Spies choreographed a number of still-popular Balinese dances, anthropologist Jane Belo (author of *Trance in Bali*), Vicki Baum (author of *A Tale of Bali*), and the Australian artists Donald Friend and Ian Fairweather. They were visited during the 1930s by such celebrities as Noël Coward, Charlie Chaplin, and Barbara Hutton, who also spread word of the island's unique charms.

It was Donald Friend who built the first house in what is now known as Batujimbar Estates and where, according to one account, he 'lived in imperial splendour with an in-house gamelan orchestra and Bali's finest art collection.' Today Batujimbar consists of a dozen or so private homes, each of which contains a tropical garden of exceptional beauty, sometimes separated by the coral walls characteristic of Balinese compounds and sometimes merging into common areas of lawn and massed beds of ornamental shrubs.

Tough native Pandanus with sharp serrated leaves has been planted along the sea wall as a protection against salty monsoon winds in a large central area overlooked by several houses, and Bougainvillea spills out of large stone containers on terraces. Shrubs with coloured foliage such as Cordylines, Codiaeums, Sanchezia, and Pseuderantheum, together with lower-growing covers like Scindapsus, Syngonium and Rhoeo, have been used in considerable quantities to provide contrasts in the beds, while shadier areas are planted with Red Ginger (Alpinia), Alocasia, Philodendron, and Maiden's Hair Fern for a jungle effect. Many of the plants at Batujimbar were first introduced to the island at the Bali Hyatt Hotel, which also overlooks Sanur Beach, by horticulturists who worked on both gardens.

Lofty coconut palms provide a backdrop for a swimming pool in the garden, fed by an artificial waterfall around which grow Philodendron and gold-leafed Scindapsus. The low plant with purple leaves in the foreground is Rhoeo.

105

A meticulously kept lawn links several gardens at Batujimbar Estate. Most of the trees were already growing on the site when the houses were built.

*B*eds of plants with coloured foliage – shrubs like Cordylines, Codiaeums, and Sanchezia and lower-growing covers like Rhoeo and Alternantheras – create islands of colour throughout the tree-dotted lawn.

*C*oconut palms, Bananas, Gingers, and other tropical specimens lend a jungle-like atmosphere to shadier portions of the estate; a native orchid grows on the trunk in the foreground.

Balinese stone carvings, created by local artisans, line a drive in the Batujimbar Estate; spilling over a wall on the right is Antigonon leptopus, *popularly known as the Chain of Love or Mexican Creeper, while the spiky plants in the foreground are Agaves.*

A guest house in the garden has been transformed into a leafy pavilion with pots of giant Maidenhair Ferns, Philodendron, and other exotics that provide screening as well as a sense of tropical luxuriance. The furniture in the background is made of giant local bamboo.

As everywhere on Bali, ponds are important features of the Batujimbar landscape design, in some cases devoted solely to pink and white lotus and in others to water hyacinth, water lettuce and papyrus. One of the swimming pools has been almost completely surrounded with tropical specimens, with a waterfall to increase its natural appearance. The houses, most of them in Balinese style with bamboo and rattan furniture, are open to allow unobstructed garden views from almost every point, and Balinese stone-carvings and lanterns are used for decoration.

Also on Sanur, just up the beach, is Tandjung Sari, a bungalow complex owned by Wiya Wawo-Runto, one of the founders of Batujimbar Estates. Established in 1962, it was one of the first resorts in the area and is still perhaps the most attractive with its series of luxuriantly planted courtyards, fern-bedecked coral walls, and extensive collection of local stone- and wood-carvings.

A Balinese stone figure in the garden of the Tandjung Sari, a bungalow complex on the beach near the Batujimbar Estate; the cloth around the figure has been presented as an offering.

*A*n open-roofed alcove planted with ferns and assorted creepers to create a private garden off the bathroom of a Tandjung Sari bungalow; a Balinese wood carving hangs on the brick wall.

A fountain in the Tandjung Sari garden, adorned with characteristic Balinese carvings and planted with Pistia, commonly called Water Lettuce.

*O*pposite: a small fishpond, fed by an artificial waterfall, is draped in a lush profusion of ferns and other tropical plants.

The Contemporary Museum Garden, Honolulu

STILL KNOWN TO OLDER RESIDENTS as 'the Spaulding estate', after the prominent family that once owned the property and made a showplace of its garden, the Contemporary Museum is located above Honolulu on Makiki Heights Drive, a site that affords panoramic views of the city. The original design of the multi-level garden has been largely retained, though new plants have been added and some of the older ones have been clipped into geometric shapes that serve as an interesting backdrop to various pieces of modern sculpture from the museum's collection displayed throughout the grounds.

The centrepiece of the garden is a sloping lawn of remarkable smoothness, dominated by an immense umbrella-shaped Rain Tree (*Samanea saman*; known in Hawaii as Monkeypod). Shaped plants in this and other areas include Natal Plum (*Carissa grandiflora*) and Surinam Cherry (*Eugenia uniflora*), both of which have dense leaves that make them well-suited for topiary. Below the lawn is a shadier, ravine-like lower garden, laid out along classic Japanese lines but also tropical in both plant material and atmosphere. Interesting ground covers are effectively used here along a rocky stream bed, among them *Selaginella umbrosa* (popularly called the Spikemoss plant), Peperomia with boldly patterned leaves, Rhoeo, and *Pilea nummularifolia* ('Creeping Charley'), while the steep hillsides are thickly planted with Anthuriums, Philodendrons, Heliconias, Ficus trees, and other exotics.

*A venerable Rain Tree (*Samanea saman*) forms its characteristic canopy over the spacious lawn of the Contemporary Museum; in the background can be seen Diamond Head and the skyscrapers of downtown Honolulu.*

Various evergreen shrubs have been clipped into geometrical shapes in the Contemporary Museum garden, enhancing pieces of sculpture from the collection and also creating a series of outdoor galleries.

A lower garden in a ravine blends Japanese landscape design with a tropical atmosphere, employing such exotics as Anthuriums and Heliconias and a wide selection of ground covers along a rocky stream bed; a Bromeliad blooms in the tree on the right.

A Bali Compound

EVER SINCE THE 1920s, when a regular steamship service was started between Bali and Java, foreigners have been attracted by the island's unique charms, and many, especially artists and scholars, have settled down for sometimes lengthy stays in Balinese homes of their own. The compound shown here, in the Sanur area, has been developed by a group of such Baliphiles, some of whom use it for holidays while others reside there more or less permanently.

Called Taman Mertasari, or 'Garden of Holy Water Essence', it contains several houses inspired by Balinese architecture as well as a traditional, thatched-roof rice barn and an open pavilion near the swimming pool. The garden, shared by all the residents, has been deliberately kept simple and open, consisting mostly of smooth lawn and tall coconut palms already on the site, with a few ornamental shrubs and hedges to provide privacy for the houses, an arrangement that requires relatively little maintenance and also allows maximum air circulation. Some palms were retained even in the large lotus pond that serves as a central feature of the compound, with earth filled in around the trunks and planted with Red Pineapple (*Ananas bracteatus*), a native of Brazil. Pathways and a terrace by the swimming pool were constructed by local artisans using slabs of volcanic stone interspersed with fine-leafed Japanese grass.

The focal point of the garden is this large pond planted with lotus, which blooms throughout most of the year in Bali; around the palm tree in the middle is planted Red Pineapple (Ananas bracteatus).

The lotus, one of the most enduring symbols in Asian art from India to China.

*A*ll of the open, Balinese-type houses in the compound have a view of the central lotus pond. The coconut palms, already growing on the site, were incorporated into the garden design.

*S*labs of volcanic stone (top right), hewn from a local quarry, are interspersed with a fine-leafed Japanese grass to form various walkways and terraces, illuminated at night by Balinese-style garden lamps.

Because of its rapidly-spreading root system, the lotus is best given a pond to itself; the flowers open in the early morning.

The Bali Hyatt Garden

EXTENDING OVER AN AREA of some 36 acres along Sanur Beach, the garden of the Bali Hyatt Hotel is the product of a number of designers going back to the hotel's completion in 1973. The architect, Kerry Hill of Australia, had planned for lush plantings and water gardens to soften the rather stark simplicity of the cement structure, and these were originally supplied by Ketut Relly, a Balinese graduate in landscape architecture from Trisakti University in Jakarta. An extensive revision was started in 1981 under the direction of Michael White, an Australian who is also known in Bali as Made Wijaya, and his associate Ketut Marsa. This consisted of altering some of the original planting and adding a Tropical Horticultural Garden composed mostly of decorative plants and occupying almost half of the front part of the grounds, as well as acquiring a collection of statuary and other objects by Balinese artists to place around the hotel courtyards and grounds.

The Bali Hyatt garden today is distinguished by a variety of imaginative plantings. Broad terraces in the front are planted with sweeping red, green, yellow, and variegated ground covers to create an effect of almost abstract designs, while courtyards in each wing of the hotel are based on theme plants like Hibiscus (in some places trained up a support to achieve heights of more than 20 feet), Bougainvillea, and Frangipani (Plumeria). Another series of terraces, leading down from the lobby to the swimming pool area, is given a dense tropical appearance by masses of Red Ginger (Alpinia) with exceptionally large flowers, Hibiscus, Acalypha, and Polyscias, with a number of lotus ponds and waterways. A windbreak of indigenous trees, Pandanus, and Plumeria is used along the sea front.

Coconut palms, their trunks almost hidden by the patterned leaves of Scindapsus, tower above a profusion of Alpinia and other tropical exotics in the densely planted area below the hotel's main terrace. Many of these plants were first introduced to Bali through the hotel garden.

A series of broad terraces at the front of the hotel, overlooking a golf course, are *planted with multi-coloured ground covers to create a sweeping, carpet-like effect.*

A *garden lamp, sheltered by a Balinese-style thatched roof (top), illuminates the pathways at night.*

*T*he *rather stark lines of the hotel are softened on* all sides by the lush garden (bottom); in this area clumps of Arundodonax versicolor, *a bamboo-like reed with variegated leaves, provide a contrast to the red-leafed ground cover; an Alpinia blooms behind.*

Several ponds, planted with both day- and night-blooming water lilies, add to the appeal of the Bali Hyatt's extensive garden. Cyperus alternifolius, *Colocasia (Taro), Swamp Fern, and other water-loving plants grow in and around the ponds.*

The Horticultural Garden, where most of the specimens are labelled, contains collections of Gingers, Heliconias, Cactus, Dracaena, Crotons, Bromeliads, water plants, and palms, as well as a special garden of plants with white flowers and/or variegated leaves designed as a sort of tropical tribute to Vita Sackville-West's famous White Garden at Sissinghurst. Lawns are studded with such flowering trees as Flamboyant (*Delonix regia*), Erythrina, and Plumeria, as well as coconut palms and shady breadfruit trees.

Aside from its aesthetic appeal to guests of the hotel, the Bali Hyatt garden has also played a significant role in the introduction of many ornamental plants to Bali. A number of Gingers, Heliconias, Plumerias and other exotics, mostly brought from Singapore and Hawaii, were first cultivated at the hotel before finding their way into gardens throughout the island, adapting so luxuriantly to the fertile soil and climate that many newcomers now mistake them for indigenous plants. A small building that serves as a Horticultural Society headquarters and library on the grounds reflects this serious and continuing botanical function.

One of the interior hotel courtyards, bringing the garden almost to the doors of the guest rooms. A Staghorn Fern hangs from the tree on the right, while below it is a Philodendron selloum; Syngonium *is used as a ground cover in the bed on the left below a Heliconia with bronze-coloured leaves.*

126

The 'White Garden' was planted as a tribute to Vita Sackville-West, the noted horticulturist of Sissinghurst fame. Most of the trees, shrubs, water plants, ground covers, and creepers in it have either white flowers or variegated leaves; growing over the trellis on the left, for instance, is a white-blooming Thunbergia grandiflora Alba, *while white water lilies bloom in the pond.*

Opposite: tough indigenous trees already growing on the site have been left along the seafront (top), where they provide shade for a pathway and protection against sea winds.

Shrubs with patterned leaves ensure continuous colour along the

garden's many walks (middle).

Carpets of colour are achieved on stepped terraces through the use of various ground covers (bottom), mostly species of Alternanthera, which requires full sun to bring out its brightest hues.

The Westin Kauai Lagoons

THE WESTIN KAUAI LAGOONS, on the island of Kauai, is one of a new collection of hotels in the USA that offer the sort of escapist fantasy usually associated with theme parks. The lobby overlooks a two-acre reflecting pool with marble fountains and live swans; launches carry guests through a series of landscaped lagoons and waterways (where six islands are stocked with exotic wildlife); three waterfalls cascade into the vast swimming pool; and $2.5 million dollars worth of Oriental and Pacific art is lavishly scattered around the public areas.

Not surprisingly in view of its location, the hotel also contains a number of well-designed garden areas that add considerably to its romantic atmosphere. Plantings in these include massed beds of Spathiphyllum and multi-coloured Impatiens, tree ferns, Cordyline, white-flowering Datura, the so-called Blue Ginger (*Dichorisandra thyrsiflora*), Bougainvillea, and assorted Hibiscus hybrids with exceptionally large flowers. Some of the smaller gardens appear to be much larger than they are through a clever use of mirrors set into the walls.

Swans glide across the water of the hotel's central pool; the marble horses that form part of the fountain were made to order in China.

Ceramic jars, set on lucite bases so that they appear to be floating, are displayed along an upper colonnade overlooking the hotel's huge swimming pool.

Hibiscus and
Plumbago are among the sun-
loving ornamentals planted in the
swimming-pool area.

Two giant
hybrid Hibiscus, of which the
hotel has a large collection
scattered through its gardens.

Impatiens, not always an easy plant to grow in the tropics, thrives in Hawaii's mild climate. Here it is used to create a multi-coloured mass in one of the Westin Kuaui's gardens.

Exposed hillsides outside the buildings and lagoon banks are carpeted with *Wedelia trilobata*, a tough ground cover popularly known as West Indian Creeper, which can withstand both sea winds and very dry conditions. On one hill is a stand of Norfolk Pines (*Araucaria heterophylla*), an evergreen tree that looks distinctly untropical though it is in fact native to the South Pacific and can be found in many hot-weather gardens.

133

*L*eft top: a Tree
Fern rises from a bed of
Spathiphyllum; the pendant white
flowers on the right are those of a
Datura, which in Kuaui
sometimes attains the height of a
small tree.

Left bottom: a marble figure of the Chinese goddess Kuan Yin is displayed beneath a Ficus tree at the hotel entrance; Spathiphyllum and Calathea are among the exotics used as a cover below, while the blue flowers in the back are Dichorisandra thyrsiflora, *popularly called the Blue Ginger though in fact it belongs to the spiderwort family.*

Hillsides around the hotel have been planted with a variety of hardy ground covers, among them Wedelia trilobata, *the West Indian Creeper. The trees are Norfolk Pines* (Araucaria heterophylla), *a native of the South Pacific.*

The Leland Miyano Garden

LOCATED IN A FERTILE AREA of frequent rainfall near the foothills of the Koolaus, one of the two spinal mountain ranges on the Hawaiian island of Oahu, Leland Miyano's garden is a one-man creation that utilizes a wide variety of plants from many parts of the tropical world. The principal source, however, has been South America and especially Brazil, where Mr Miyano has gone on a number of collecting trips with his close friend and mentor Roberto Burle-Marx, the noted landscape designer responsible for many of the finest Brazilian gardens.

The Miyano garden covers only about an acre but seems much larger thanks to a creative design that utilizes winding pathways and massed plantings on hillocks and offers a series of surprising new vistas at each turn. Burle-Marx's influence is evident in the beds of swirling colour, largely provided by the showy bracts of Bromeliads and Cordylines, or Ti plants as they are known in Hawaii, in shades that range from ruby-red to flaming orange. Also outstanding are the numerous Philodendrons Mr Miyano has brought back from the South American jungles, some so recent to domestic cultivation that they have not yet been named, and a large collection of Cycads, among the oldest of the world's plants, in which he has a particular interest.

Additional noteworthy specimens used in the garden include several kinds of Heliconia, a variety of tropical iris planted around a lily pond, shrub species of both white- and purple-flowering Petrea (normally found as a creeper), a number of unusual orchids planted on rocks and tree trunks, a rare Mussaenda from Brazil with star-shaped red flowers, a Mimosa with striking cinnamon-coloured bark, and an assortment of unusual ground covers employed in effective masses along the pathways.

Bromeliads with brightly coloured leaves have been used as a ground cover in this part of the Leland Miyano garden. The large plant in the background is a self-heading Philodendron from Brazil, while below it are some of the Cycads from Mr Miyano's large collection. A lotus grows in the water jar along with Water Lettuce (Pistia).

137

Colour and varied leaf textures are provided by tall Cordylines, a silvery Coccothrinax argentata palm, assorted Bromeliads, and, on the right, two unusual Brazilian Philodendrons. Mr Miyano uses no chemical fertilizers or pesticides in his garden, relying entirely on natural methods.

138

A tropical iris blooms on the bank of a pond, top; on the far side is a white-flowering Tabernaemontana, which resembles a small gardenia though without the strong scent, and assorted Bromeliads.

A mixture of Bromeliads, bottom left, with foliage of varying size and colour; the fern-like plants behind are Cycas.

*L*ow-growing Cordylines, bottom right, useful as a colourful ground cover.

*Bromeliads,
Cycas, Cordylines and
Philodendrons growing around a
small pool; a tufted, grass-like
ground cover is in the foreground.
The influence of Roberto Burle-
Marx, the well-known Brazilian
landscape architect and a friend
of Mr Miyano's, is apparent in
the use of brightly coloured plants
and ground covers to create
artistic patterns in the garden.*

In addition to the sunny main garden, there is also a sunken area that simulates humid jungle conditions through dense plantings of bananas, palms, and larger Heliconias; here Mr Miyano germinates many of the seeds he brings back from his collecting trips, especially palms, nurturing the young plants until they are ready to be tried out in other places.

A serious plant collector who has introduced a large number of new ornamentals to Hawaii, Mr Miyano is also a practising landscape designer and the garden he has achieved, largely without assistance, functions as a showcase for useful ideas in both general layout and harmonious plantings. He is a firm believer, incidentally, in the principles of organic gardening and uses neither pesticides nor chemical fertilizers in his own.

Opposite: a tree in the courtyard becomes a showcase for an impressive variety of tropical exotics, among them Stag Horn Ferns, Bromeliads, and an Anthurium with large, splendidly patterned leaves.

An unusual Mussaenda from Brazil.

Brassavola Digbyana; *the red leaves are Bromeliads.*

Pitcairnia *species (collected by Roberto Burle-Marx).*

Brassavola *orchids blooming in the midst of a clump of rare Aechmea Bromeliads (below left).*

Epiphytic *orchids and Bromeliads planted on rocks in one corner of the garden; in the background are Cycas and Cordylines.*

*Behind a
planting of Bromeliads, sprays of
Oncidium orchid flowers add a
bright splash of gold; in the
background are richly-coloured
Cordylines and the fern-like
leaves of a Cycad (left, top).*

An assortment of
low-growing plants provides
contrasting textures throughout
the garden, sets off the distinctive
shapes of larger plants, and helps
the soil retain moisture in dry
periods (left, below).

*R*hoeo is used as
an effective ground cover along
this stone pathway, while the
spiky leaves of Bromeliads and
Cycads give colour and height to
the landscape. The long feathery
leaves in the background on the
right are those of a 'Pony-tail
Palm' (Beaucarnea recurvata).

145

Striking patterns are created through the careful use of varicoloured ground covers. On the left in the background is a giant Cycad, one of the earliest plants to appear on earth, while on the right is a pair of Traveler's Palms (Ravenala), a native of Madagascar which acquired its popular name because fresh water collects at the bases of the leaves and can be drunk by thirsty wanderers.

The Allerton Gardens

KAUAI, HAWAII'S OLDEST POPULATED ISLAND, is a place of dramatic volcanic scenery and climatic contrast. Waialeale, at its eastern end, is known as the wettest spot on earth, with an annual rainfall of some 500 inches, while the western side is almost desert at higher elevations; a number of the native birds and plants on Kauai are found nowhere else in the islands, thanks to sanctuaries provided by high mountains and dense jungle canyons, and it is ringed with sandy beaches of exceptional beauty.

The Allerton gardens, located in a verdant valley on the west coast, were started by Queen Emma, wife of King Kamehameha IV, who lived on the picturesque seaside site until 1875. An enthusiastic gardener, Queen Emma introduced a large number of ornamental specimens to the island, including a mass planting of Bougainvillea which cascades down a cliff behind the present house. After her death, the property was acquired by Alexander McBryde, a noted horticulturist, who enlarged the plant collection and laid out the garden along its present lines.

Coconut palms shade the lawn of the Allerton house, behind which lie the gardens created by Robert Allerton and his son John Gregg Allerton over a span of some fifty years.

149

Scarlet
Clerodendron flowers add colour
to one of the densely planted
pathways on a hillside;
Philodendrons climb in the trees
above and form a cover on the
slope.

In 1938 the lower end of the Lawai valley, which includes the property, was purchased by Robert Allerton, originally as a winter home. His son John designed the house and together with his father travelled widely to collect more plants; they also added a number of pools, waterfalls, and architectural features to the gardens. After inheriting the estate, John Gregg Allerton continued to improve the extensive gardens and lived there until his own death in 1989. The property, now under the supervision of Mr Toshi Kaneko, who worked with Mr Allerton for many years, was bequeathed to the adjoining Pacific Tropical Botanical Gardens, whose aims include the preservation of endangered tropical plants and research into species of medicinal and economic value.

Lawai Kai, as the gardens are called, covers a large area on both sides of a wide stream flowing through the valley to the sea, and enjoys an unusually varied topography that includes open meadows, moist jungled ravines, and hills rising to considerable heights. These, together with Kauai's rich volcanic soil, offer ideal growing conditions to a wide selection of plants and trees and made

*T*his elongated
shallow pool, on several different
levels, is one of the several
striking water features in the
Allerton gardens.

151

*T*he Mermaid
Fountain empties into an Art
Deco zigzag channel, making an
imaginative artistic statement
against the tropical mass of
Rhapis palms. The mermaid
figures are identified as having
been made by a Florentine
sculptor named Andreotti in 1931.

*O*verleaf
(pp.154–155): a serene, latticed
pavilion overlooks the Diana
Fountain on one of the garden's
upper levels. Most of the statuary
was acquired by the Allertons on
trips to Europe.

it possible for the Allertons to create a garden – more precisely, a series of gardens linked by pathways – of imaginative design and exceptional botanical interest. One section, for instance, is largely devoted to an impressive collection of Heliconias, Costus, Calathea, and Gingers while another contains mainly different species of giant bamboo. Hillsides are planted with either Cassias of assorted hues (known as Shower Trees in Hawaii, where they are frequently used to line streets) or varied Plumerias, and on the exposed cliff overlooking the sea are cacti (including a low wall of night-blooming Cereus) and Bougainvillea.

     Scattered throughout in strategic clearings, the gazebos, pools, fountains, and statuary (which ranges from classical to Art Deco) add to the charm of Lawai Kai without detracting from the generally natural atmosphere that gives it such distinction.

*Y*ellow Bamboo (Phyllostachys) *creates a dimly lit forest in an area devoted to various species of Bamboo. Elsewhere in the garden are comprehensive collections of other tropical plants and flowering trees.*

The twisted roots of aged Ficus trees form odd patterns near the top of a towering cliff in the Allerton gardens.

Perpetually dripping water creates an ideal environment for a wall of ferns, moss, and tropical creepers along a road leading to the upper reaches of the gardens.

Giant Anthuriums border a stream that cascades over successive levels down a hillside; thanks to such features the restful sound of running water is audible in almost every part of the extensive gardens.

The Victor Sassoon Garden

In the foreground can be seen the huge leaves and a freshly opened flower of Victoria Amazonica, *the great Brazilian water lily that became the rage of Victorian England when one flowered in a special glasshouse at Chatsworth. Beyond, a lawn of Malaysian grass leads to the rear terrace of the Sassoon house.*

VICTOR SASSOON'S GARDEN – an unusually large one for a private compound in present-day Bangkok – has been developed over some 25 years. Trees, coconut and fishtail palms, and tall stands of bamboo provide an effective screen on three sides of the property, creating a rare green oasis in a residential district now largely dominated by impersonal high-rise condominiums.

Already on the site, mostly near the house, were a number of mature trees, among them Mango, Tamarind, and Flamboyant (*Delonix regia*), and to these have been added *Tabebuia rosea, Pterocarpus indica, Lagerstroemia floribunda,* and *Peltophorum inerme* (Yellow Poinciana). Flowering shrubs and exotics planted in beds include several species of Hibiscus, dwarf Ixora (trimmed to form a hedge along the drive), varied Heliconias, *Sanchezia nobilis,* Spathiphyllum, Dieffenbachia, and assorted Philodendrons, while among the creepers on fences and trellises are Bougainvillea, *Petrea volubilis, Thunbergia grandiflora, Cleloden-dron splendens,* and *Solandra nitida.* A large L-shaped pond at the rear of the garden contains *Victoria Amazonica* as well as smaller water lilies in various colours. On a terrace, potted plants – among them large hybrid Spathiphylum, Maidenhair ferns, Hibiscus, Bougainvillea, and Heliconias with showy green-and-yellow leaves – have been massed to create a luxuriant tropical atmosphere reflecting that of the garden as a whole.

Spathiphyllums provide a setting for an antique water jar used as decoration in the garden.

*P*otted ferns and
assorted foliage plants bring the garden
onto the terrace near the front
entrance, shaded by a Mango tree.

Heliconia
illustris, *grown for its colourful
leaves rather than its flowers
(left), adds to the colour of the*

terrace pot plants; on the right is
a hybrid Spathiphyllum which
has exceptionally large blooms. In
the background is an aviary.

*D*warf Ixora has
been clipped to form a neat hedge
along the driveway. Solandra
guttata, *popularly called the Cup*

of Gold, grows over the trellis,
while a mass of Heliconias is on
the right. The tree shading the
area is a Ficus benchamina.

Bangkok Hilton International Garden

THE HILTON INTERNATIONAL HOTEL IN BANGKOK was built partly on the site of a pleasure garden created in the early years of this century by a prominent businessman named Nai Lert; the area was then on the outskirts of the city, accessible only by canal, and the garden, popularly known as Nai Lert Park, was used as a weekend retreat. When Nai Lert's daughter, Khunying Lurasakdi Sampati-siri, decided to develop the property in the mid-1980s, she redesigned a part of the park and incorporated it into the hotel grounds, creating one of the largest semi-private gardens in central Bangkok today.

Water is a prominent feature of the garden, with two ponds – the larger planted with *Victoria Amazonica* water lilies – and an artificial waterfall of impressive dimensions. Most of the plants came from Khunying Lurasakdi's own large collection and include an unusually wide variety of trees, shrubs, climbers, and ground covers, most labelled with their Thai and botanical names. Among the flowering trees are Jacaranda, Delonix (including one with unusual apricot-coloured flowers), both white- and red-blooming Erythrina, Bauhinia (Orchid Tree), *Peltophorum inerme* (Yellow Poinciana), *Saraca indica*, Plumeria, Tabebuia, and several kinds of Cassia, one of which (*C. fistula*, or Golden Shower) is Thailand's national tree. Shady areas are planted with Philodendron, ferns, and various foliage plants, while such shrubs as Ixora (in red, pink, white, and orange), Oleander, Hibiscus, Lantana, Jasmine, and Gardenia grow in sunnier parts. Climbers include *Petrea volubilis*, with purple sprays that resemble Wisteria; Bougainvillea in assorted colours; *Beaumontia grandiflora*, which has huge clusters of fragrant white flowers; and a climbing Bauhinia with white flowers and fern-like leaves.

Spacious in size, the Hilton International garden nonetheless manages to suggest the intimate atmosphere of a personal creation, thus preserving a link with its origins nearly a century ago.

Ordinary water lilies and, in the background, the giant Victoria Amazonica *grow in the main pond of the Hilton garden. On the opposite bank is a large* Pandanus sanderi *with variegated leaves.*

165

A bridge spans one of the garden's waterways, beneath a canopy of coconut palms and flowering trees.

Bixa orellana, *popularly called the Lipstick Plant.*

Acalypha hispida, *the Chenille Plant.*

An artificial waterfall, shaded by a small jungle of Ficus trees and Bamboo, forms one of the most striking landscape features in the Hilton garden.

Garden Features

A modern Thai earthenware jar used as a garden ornament.

Courtyard of the Hart and Tagami Gallery in Hawaii.

In tropical as in temperate gardens, the ultimate success of a landscape design depends not only on the selection and arrangement of plant materials but also on the skill with which assorted features are employed to enhance its natural beauty. A path or walkway of unusual design and texture, a fence or wall that manages to be attractive as well as practical, a strategically sited gazebo, an imaginative use of statuary and lighting fixtures, ornamental fountains, pools, or even extensive artificial lakes — all can be vital in creating the special atmosphere that makes a particular garden memorable.

Pathways

WALKWAYS ARE NOT ONLY ESSENTIAL to most garden designs but also add to — or in some cases detract from — their overall effectiveness. An interesting pattern of bricks or other material can turn a path into more than simply a means of getting from one part of the landscape to another, just as it can give character to a poolside terrace or courtyard; on the other hand, the unimaginative use of cement can destroy what might otherwise be a pleasing view or atmosphere. Of equal importance is the choice of plants that border such obviously man-made features, either disguising and softening the edges or giving them emphasis.

Sections of a tree trunk are used as stepping stones in a garden in northern Thailand.

Pathways at the Amandari Hotel in Bali form interesting geometric patterns as they cross a courtyard. The garden was designed by Made Wijaya.

*P*ebbles and larger stones form swirling designs in the courtyard of the Han Snel Guest House in Ubud, Bali; a hanging Heliconia blooms against the wall in the background.

A pathway in the garden of Bangkok's Oriental Hotel.

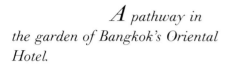

A rustic path, bordered by a variegated ground cover, in Java's Cibodas Botanical Garden.

A patterned brick walkway in a Malaysian resort.

Garden Ornaments

THE VARIETY OF STRUCTURES, statuary, and other decorative garden features is almost endless, with the choice depending mainly on individual taste. Larger areas can accommodate an ornamental pavilion, orchid house, or aviary, while almost any landscape can be improved through strategically sited stone, wood, metal, or ceramic figures, large water jars planted with lilies or displayed merely as objects of beauty, garden furniture of pleasing and harmonious design, and distinctive works of art that reflect local culture or that are created especially for the space in which they are used.

Opposite: an antique Chinese statue; a ceramic fish made in northeastern Thailand; a stone figure of the Hindu god Ganesha.

A northern-style Thai spirit house in the Bangkok garden of Mr and Mrs Yvan Van Outrive.

A Thai-style pavilion built over a pond in a Bangkok garden.

Ornamental figure in Singapore's Botanical Garden.

Painted water jars at the Oriental Hotel's Chinese restaurant.

Glazed tiles set in the wall of a Singapore garden.

Sunken jars used for growing water lilies.

Against a luxuriant background of Heliconia, an antique water jar is used as a container for Nymphaea; placed with shells and coral on the stone on the left is an earthenware Thai jar.

A huge, elegantly-shaped 14th-century water jar from Sukhothai, the first Thai capital, serves as a dramatic focal point on a lawn containing various palms in a Bangkok garden.

Walls and Fences

IF WALLS AND FENCES do not make for good neighbours, such barriers are nonetheless necessary in most gardens, tropical or otherwise, not only to delineate property but also to screen out certain areas. They can be enhanced in a number of ways, however: by almost covering them with a luxuriant display of plants, by building on a series of levels so that the wall becomes a part of the garden, or, perhaps most common of all, by accentuating them through the use of imaginative materials – bamboo, for instance, or coral, as in the case of most Balinese walls, or with insets of ceramic tiles – to create a pleasing architectural pattern.

A stone wall planted with assorted Bromeliads at the Kahala Hilton Hotel in Honolulu.

178

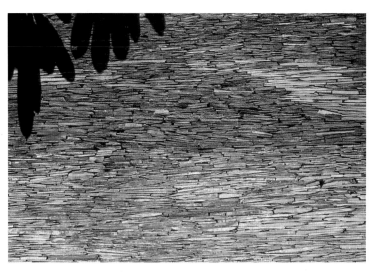

Ⅎicus pumila *creeps across a wall of closely fitted stones.*

𝐴 *Balinese wall made with thin slabs of volcanic stone.*

𝐴 *patterned wall made of coral in a Balinese garden.*

𝑀*exican Creeper* (Antigonon leptopus) *on a wall of black coral.*

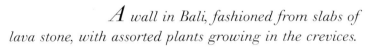

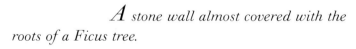

𝐴 *wall in Bali, fashioned from slabs of lava stone, with assorted plants growing in the crevices.*

𝐴 *stone wall almost covered with the roots of a Ficus tree.*

*P*ierced, glazed Chinese tiles create an interesting decorative pattern, and also allow air circulation, when incorporated into a wall like this one in Bali.

A fence of bamboo in contrasting patterns serves as a screen as well as a decorative feature in the garden of Bangkok's Oriental Hotel; a modern Thai jar is on the left.

*R*ustic fences of split bamboo, at once attractive and inexpensive, are commonly seen in rural Thailand; this one is in a garden in the northern town of Lampang.

A trim white wooden fence borders a flight of steps leading down a steep hillside to a garden in Honolulu; the walls are thickly covered with Ficus pumila.

A massive effect is created by a wall made of cement and volcanic stone bordering a walkway at Bali's Amandari Hotel, designed by Australian architect Peter Muller.

Pools, Fountains, and Waterfalls

WHETHER MODEST OR SPECTACULAR, ornamental pools, fountains, and waterfalls have been a prominent part of tropical gardens since antiquity and continue to be so today. A decorative pool may be severely formal, an architectural extension of the buildings around it, or natural-looking with carefully selected rocks and plants, while fountains can be fashioned from a wide variety of objects as suggested in those shown here. Similarly, the restful sound of water cascading down over different levels can be achieved even without topography through ingenious methods that disguise their artificiality.

An unusual fountain made of stacked ceramic pots, in a northern Thai garden; formal, clipped plants, a traditional Thai specialty, are in the background.

An old grindstone, once used by Chinese who came to work in local tin mines, forms the base of a fountain in the Ault Garden at Phuket; water power is supplied by a stream flowing through the property.

A series of pools, one flowing into
another, in the garden of M.L. Tri Devakul at Phuket.

*A*n artificial waterfall, spilling into a
pool of ornamental carp, in the garden of the Prasart
Museum in Bangkok.

*Khmer figures in
a geometric pond in the garden of
M.R. Kukrit Pramoj in Bangkok.*

*A pond bordered
by slabs of laterite, planted with
tall, blue-flowering Thalia
geniculata, lotus, Nymphaea, and
other specimens, all in pots.*

*A formal pool in
which lotus and water lilies are
combined, adorned by an antique
Chinese stone figure.*

A pond for assorted water plants off the terrace of a house in Bali.

An informal pool with rocks and an artificial waterfall at the Kahala Hilton Hotel.

Swimming Pools

SERVING BOTH AS WATER FEATURES and as places for family recreation, swimming pools are incorporated into garden designs throughout the tropics. Some, especially those in hotel gardens, are of impressive size and imaginative configuration; the pool at the Amandari Hotel in Bali, for instance, follows the irregular form of rice terraces that spill dramatically into a valley far below, while others are built around luxuriantly planted little islands; even standard rectangular pools can be given an individual distinction through the use of unusual fountains or large containers planted with flowering shrubs and creepers.

Swimming pool of the Amandari Hotel at Ubud in Bali.

Natural rocks are incorporated into the pool at the Pelangi Resort in Langkawi, Malaysia.

A salt-water pool in Phuket, built in the rocks overlooking the Andaman Sea.

A pool in a garden in Bali, softened by a dense tropical planting.

A fountain of black stone covered with small Bromeliads supplies water for a Hawaiian garden pool.

Opposite: a pool overlooking the Pacific Ocean in Honolulu; pink Mussaenda blooms on the left, white Plumeria on the right.

Tropical Plants

*G*round covers in varying colours and leaf forms, on sale at a Bangkok plant market.

A densely planted bed of Spathiphyllum.

*'I*t takes a little time', a visitor to the tropics once wrote, 'for the temperate mind to accept the palm-tree as a common, natural, and inevitable object in every outlook and landscape.' The same applies to the countless other ornamentals familiar to many only as delicate specimens to be carefully nurtured under artificial conditions but available as ordinary plant materials to the tropical gardener. Creepers and ground covers, shrubs and flowering trees, exotics with flamboyantly coloured bracts and patterned leaves of incredible complexity – the range is vast and the landscape opportunities almost limitless.

191

Heliconias and Gingers

SOME OF THE MOST BRILLIANT splashes of colour in contemporary tropical gardens are provided by the Heliconia and Ginger families, both of which have relatively insignificant flowers but extremely visible bracts.

Natives of tropical America, the Heliconia family includes about 80 species, ranging in size from dwarfs only a few feet tall to towering giants as large as their close relation, the banana. Most have colourful red, orange, yellow, or pink bracts, sometimes standing erect and sometimes hanging in striking clusters. Similarly exotic in appearance – and once classified as part of the same botanical family – is Strelitzia, the beautiful Bird of Paradise, which has either blue-and-orange or blue-and-white flowers.

The Gingers are equally varied, consisting of 45 genera and some 700 species. Among the most popular with tropical gardeners are the Red Ginger (*Alpinia purpurata*), with ruby-coloured bracts; the Shell Ginger (*Alpinia zerumbet*), which has long clusters of pink corollas and yellow and red flowers; and the Torch Ginger (*Nicolaia elatior*, also known as *Phaeomeria magnifica*), on which the red or pink waxy bracts rise straight out of the ground.

Nicolaia elatior, *the Torch Ginger*

Opposite (top): Alpinia sanderae;
　　Dichorisandra thyrsiflora, 'Blue Ginger'
Middle: Tapeinochilus ananassae,
　　'Indonesian Ginger'; Alpinia purpurata,
　　'Red Ginger'
Bottom: Strelitzia reginae; Strelitzia nicolai

Heliconia stricta

Flowering Banana (Musa)

Shell Ginger (Alpinia nutans)

Heliconia latisphatha, left
Heliconia caribaea, *right*

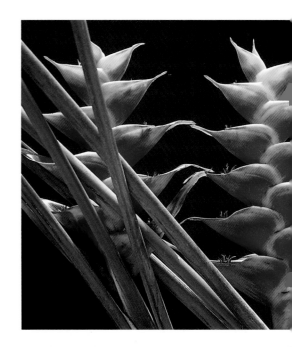

Heliconia wagneriana, *left*
Heliconia caribaea, *right*

Heliconia psittacorum, *left*
Heliconia trichocarpa, *right*

Opposite:
Tapeinochilus, *top left*
Etlingera speciosa, *top right*
Calathea *sp., middle left*
Costus hybrid, middle right
Musa acuminata, *bottom left*
Heliconia mariae, *'Beefsteak*
    Heliconia', bottom right

195

Foliage Plants

MANY TROPICAL GARDENERS FACE THE CHALLENGE of providing colour in places without a dry, blooming season or in garden areas that lack adequate sunlight. This can be easily achieved with the numerous exotic plants on which the foliage rather than the flowers are the main attraction.

Often-used foliage plants that do well in sunny or semi-shaded plantings include Cordyline (the Hawaiian Ti plant), in colours that range from bronze to bright red; numerous species of Dracaena, both large and small; Codiaeum (Croton), in an almost infinite variety of subtle designs; Acalypha, with reddish-brown, copper, or variegated leaves; and *Sanchezia nobilis*, which has green leaves with bright yellow veins. Variety can be brought to shady areas with a selection of Dieffenbachia or Aglaonema hybrids, in endless complex combinations of green and white; a wide selection of Maranta and Calathea; several species of Anthurium, Alcocasia, and Philodendron with leaf patterns that resemble an abstract painting; and Caladium, the ever-popular house plant of temperate countries which in the tropics can be used to brighten a jungle-garden pathway.

Opposite:
Leaves of Hibiscus rosa-sinensis 'cooperi', *top left*
Amaranthus tricolour, top right
Amaranthus tricolour, middle left
Caladium, bottom left
Dieffenbachia amoena, *'Tropic Snow', bottom right*

Hibiscus rosa-sinensis
with variegated leaves

Acalypha wilkesiana, *'Fire Dragon'*

Strobilantes dyerianus, *'Persian shield'*

Codiaeum variegatum

Codiaeum variegatum

198

Cordyline hybrid

Codiaeum variegatum

Variegated Schefflera

Anthurium crystallinum

Flowering Shrubs

THE RANGE OF CLIMATES AND SOIL conditions in the tropics – far greater than many realize – determines the equally wide variety of flowering shrubs that may be grown in a garden. Some demand a prolonged dry spell to produce satisfactory blooms, others at least a few months of relatively cool weather, a certain elevation, or a particular soil; nearly all require good drainage and adequate sunlight.

A traditional favourite in most localities is the Hibiscus – now, thanks to continued hybridization, available in numerous forms and colours, from small single blossoms to giant doubles. Also popular are Ixora, regular-sized or dwarf, with red, orange, pink, yellow, or white flowers; Mussaenda, a native of the Philippines with regular masses of cream or pink sepals; Plumbago, one of the rare sources of blue flowers; Caesalpinia, which has almost continual orange, yellow, or strawberry-coloured blooms; the drought-resistant Adenium; and a shrub variety of Allamanda, which thrives in sandy areas near the sea. Fragrance, strongest in the evening, is provided by *Cestrum nocturnum*, assorted species of Jasminum, *Murraya paniculata* ('Mock Orange'), Gardenia, and Michelia.

Hibiscus siriacus

Shrub variety of Allamanda

200

Hibiscus hybrid, top left
Hibiscus hybrid, top right
Hibiscus hybrid, second row, left
Hibiscus rosa-sinensis, *second row, right*
Cordia, third row, left
Baleria, third row, right
Pachystachys lutea, *bottom row, left*
Adenium obesum, *bottom row, right*

201

Euphorbia (Poinsettia)

Warszewiczia coccinea

Opposite:
Ixora macrothyrsa, *top left*
Bixa orellana, *top right*
Ixora hybrid, middle left
Mussaenda philippica, *middle right*
Ixora hybrid, bottom left
Medinilla magnifica, *bottom right*

Water Plants

MANY TROPICAL GARDENS have some sort of decorative water feature, ranging from small pools to sizable lakes and canals, and these in turn are usually further enhanced with ornamental plants. For best results the water should be relatively shallow, not more than three or four feet in depth, and care must be taken in selecting fish that will not eat the plant material.

The multi-coloured water lilies of the Nymphaea family are popular for obvious reasons, and a really large pond can accommodate *Victoria Amazonica*, that huge favourite of the great 19th-century glasshouses; the lotus, on the other hand, tends to spread too rapidly and is best either grown in pots or given a pool to itself. Floating plants good for small ponds and containers include the Water Poppy (*Hydrocleis nymphoides*), Water Lettuce (Pistia), and the beautiful Water Hyacinth (Eichhornia). Pond edges can be softened with plantings of Cyperus, which comes in a number of varieties including the well-known Papyrus; *Thalia geniculata*, popularly called the Water Canna, with dangling clusters of mauve flowers; and Pandanus, available in large and small species, some with handsome yellow-and-green striped leaves and dramatic root formations.

Nelumbo nucifera

Victoria Amazonica

Nymphaea sp.

Nymphaea sp.

Nymphaea 'Tashkent'

Nymphaea sp.

Nymphaea sp.

Nymphaea sp.

Fishtail ferns and a Pandanus sanderi with variegated leaves in the garden of Suan Pakkad Palace, Bangkok.

Cyperus alternifolius, Calocasia (Taro), and Nymphaea (opposite, top).

Water hyacinth, Cyperus, and Pistia (Water Lettuce) in a carp pond (bottom).

206

Vines and Creepers

THE TROPICAL WORLD OFFERS an abundance of ornamental vines and creepers to adorn garden trellises and glorify otherwise mundane walls and fences.

Originally from Brazil but now found in almost every warm-weather country, the versatile Bougainvillea is available in a wide spectrum of hues ranging from purple and crimson – the hardiest varieties – to pale mauve and pure white; some hybrids have two colours on the same plant, while others have impressive displays of frilly double bracts or variegated leaves. Tropical America is also the source of Allamanda, with bright yellow tubular blossoms; *Solandra gutta*, popularly known as the Cup of Gold because of its huge pale-yellow scented flowers; and such members of the Bignonia family as the dazzling Orange Trumpet and the decorative but odiferous Garlic Vine. Two spectacular natives of Southeast Asia are the Jade Vine (*Stronglodon macrobotrys*) and the New Guinea Creeper (*Mucuna bennettii*), the former with hanging clusters of blue-green flowers and the latter with similar bright red-orange displays, while the now widespread Rangoon Creeper (*Quisqualis indica*), with masses of red, pink, and white flowers, was first cultivated in India.

Quisqualis indica, *'Rangoon Creeper'*

Pseudocalymma alliaceum, *'Garlic Vine'*

Strophanthus gratus

Solandra nitida, *'Cup of Gold', left*
Allamanda, right

Mucuna bennettii, *'New Guinea*
Creeper'

Bougainvillea

Opposite:
Bougainvillea spectabilis, *top left*
Bougainvillea glabra, *top right*
Bougainvillea hybrids, middle left
Bougainvillea spectabilis, *bottom left*
Antigonon leptopus, *bottom right*

Ground Covers

GROUND COVERS SERVE a practical purpose by discouraging weeds and preventing soil from washing away during heavy rains, particularly on slopes; they can also be put to highly decorative uses, linking taller plants in a bed or providing dramatic sweeps of contrasting colour in the manner of Brazil's garden designer Roberto Burle-Marx.

Popular covers for sunny or semi-shaded areas include Alternanthera, a native of Brazil which comes in red, pink, and variegated forms and rapidly achieves a carpet effect; assorted creeping Lanatas with purple, pink, yellow, and white flowers; Rhoeo, with spiky leaves that are bronzy-green on top and reddish-purple below; Portulaca in numerous bright colours; and a variety of ornamental Coleus. Shady places can be covered with Zebrina, which has striking grey-green stripes on a purple background; Episcia, with furry leaves in a wide range of patterns and colours; fast-growing Scindapsus and Philodenrons, with variegated, marble-like leaves in combinations of green, white, and yellow; glossy-leafed Peperomia, sometimes with intricate designs; or various kinds of Selaginella, which spread extensively in moist areas.

Portulaca grandiflora, *top*
Creeping Lantana, middle
Begonia, bottom left

Mixed ground covers: Ferns, Peperomia, Episcia, Maranta

Peperomia vershaffeltii

Peperomia glabella variegata

Peperomias

Hemigraphis colorata

Fitonia

Selaginella

214

Rhoeo

Dwarf Pandanus

Episcia cupreata

Philodendron

Impatiens

At top, Portulaca;
left Senecio;
bottom and right, Alternanthera

215

Flowering Trees

THE CHOICE OF FLOWERING TREES available to a tropical gardener is vast, the main limiting factor being the amount of space available for planting. A small garden may be able to accommodate only two or three medium-sized specimens, while larger ones can enjoy the luxury of park-like planting and blooms spaced out over much of the year.

Among the moderate-sized trees are several that are almost emblematic of the tropics: the fragrant Plumeria, in colours that range from pure white with a yellow centre to rich crimson; Cassias (Shower Trees), in bright gold, pink, white, apricot, and assorted mixtures; the Bauhinia, or Orchid Tree; several members of the Tabebuia family, some with pink blooms, others with bright yellow; and Spathodea, the African Tulip tree, on which the flowers appear in bright orange-gold clusters. Requiring more space are such standards as *Delonix regia* (popularly known as the Flame Tree in some places, as the Flamboyant in others), with its annual masses of brilliant red-orange blossoms; *Saraca indica*, with scented orange flowers; and *Samanea saman* (the Rain Tree or Monkeypod) which, properly grown, takes a splendid umbrella shape.

Bauhinia purpurea, *'Orchid Tree'*

216

Tabebuia argentea, *top left*
Cassia javanica, *top right*
Delonix regia, *middle right*
Cassia fistula, *'Golden Shower Tree', bottom left*
Cassia hybrid, 'Shower Tree', bottom right

Plumeria rubra, *'Frangipani'*

Bauhinia purpurea, *'Orchid Tree',*
  top left
Flowering Saraca indica *tree, top right*
Plumeria acutifolia, *middle left*
Brassaia actinophylla, *'Octopus Tree',*
  bottom left
Spathodea campanulata, *'African
  Tulip Tree', bottom right*

Bibliography

AMRANAND, PIMSAI *Gardening in Bangkok.* The Siam Society, Bangkok, 1976.

BASHAM, A.L. *The Wonder that was India.* Fontana Books, New Delhi, 1981

BRUGGEMAN, L. *Tropical Plants and Their Cultivation.* Thames and Hudson, London, 1957.

CLAY, HORACE F. and HUBBARD, JAMES C. *The Hawai'i Garden: Tropical Exotics.* University Press of Hawaii, Honolulu, 1977.

EISEMAN, FRED and MARGARET *Flowers of Bali.* Periplus Editions, Berkeley, 1988.

GILLILAND, H.B. *Common Malayan Plants.* University of Malaya Press, Kuala Lumpur, 1958.

GRAF, ALFRED BIRD *Tropica, Color Cyclopedia of Exotic Plants and Trees.* Roehrs Company, New Jersey, 1978.

GREENSILL, T.M. *Gardening in the Tropics.* Evans Brothers Ltd., London, 1964.

HARGREAVES, DOROTHY and BOB *Hawaii Blossoms.* Hargreaves Industrial, Portland, Oregon, 1958.

HEPPER, J. NIGEL (ed.) *Kew, Gardens for Science and Pleasure.* Her Majesty's Stationery Office, London, 1982.

HOLTUM, R.E. *Gardening in the Lowlands of Malaya.* Straits Times Press, Singapore, 1953.

HYAMS, EDWARD and MACQUITTY, WILLIAM *Great Botanical Gardens of the World.* Thomas Nelson and Sons, London, 1969.

JELLICOE, GEOFFREY and SUSAN (ed.) *The Oxford Companion to Gardens.* Oxford University Press, Oxford, 1986.

KUCK, LORAINE E. and TONGG, RICHARD C. *Hawaiian Flowers and Flowering Trees.* Charles E. Tuttle Company, Tokyo, 1960.

MCMAKIN, PATRICK D. *A Field Guide to the Flowering Plants of Thailand.* White Lotus Co. Ltd., Bangkok, 1988.

MACMILLAN, H.F. *Tropical Planting and Gardening.* Macmillan and Company, London, 1935.

MENNINGER, EDWIN A. *Flowering Trees of the World.* Hearthside Press, New York, 1962.

MERRILL, ELMER D. *Plant Life of the Pacific World.* Charles E. Tuttle Company, Tokyo, 1981.

MOIR, MAY A. *The Garden Watcher.* Harold L. Lyon Arboretum, University of Hawaii, Honolulu, 1983.

PICKELL, DAVID (ed.) *Bali, Island of the Gods.* Periplus Editions, Inc., Berkeley, 1990.

POLUNIN, IVAN *Plants and Flowers of Singapore.* Times Editions, Singapore, 1987.

SAVAGE, VICTOR R. *Western Impressions of Nature and Landscape in Southeast Asia.* Singapore University Press, Singapore, 1984.

SCIDMORE, E.R. *Java, The Garden of the East.* Oxford University Press, Singapore, 1984.

STEINER, DR. MONA LISA *Philippine Ornamental Plants.* Carmeno and Bauermann Inc., Manila, 1960.

THOMAS, ARTHUR *Gardening in Hot Countries.* Faber and Faber, London, 1965.

TINSLEY, BONNIE *Visions of Delight: The Singapore Botanic Gardens through the Ages.* Singapore Botanic Gardens, Singapore, 1989.

WHITTLE, TYLER *The Plant Hunters.* Heinemann, London, 1970.

Acknowledgments

This book would not have been possible without the generous assistance of many people in a variety of countries. The author and photographer wish particularly to thank the following:

Mr Putu Aryasuta of the Bali Hyatt Hotel, Mr and Mrs John Ault, Mr Joop Ave, Director General of Tourism for the Republic of Indonesia, Mrs Cobey Black, Mr Bernard Brack of the Bangkok Hilton International Hotel, Mr and Mrs Paul Cassiday, Mr Manop Charoensuk, Mrs Gerald Corbett, Ms Nancy Daniels of the Kahala Hilton Hotel, M.L. Tri Devakul, Ms Trina Dingler Ebert of Aman Resorts, Mr and Mrs John Ede of the Mandai Gardens, Ms Cheryl Engstrom of the Westin Kauai Hotel, Dr Fritz A. Frauchiger of the Contemporary Museum in Honolulu, Mrs Sue Girson, Mr Rio Helmi, Mr Brent Hesselyn, Ms Henrietta Ho of the Hyatt Hotel Group, Mr Tan Jiew Hoe, Mr and Mrs Hans Hofer, Ms Stephanie Kaluahine-Reid of the Westin Kauai Hotel, Mr Toshi Kaneko of the Allerton Gardens, Dr Tan Wee Kiat of the Singapore Botanic Gardens, Mr Sunny Khoo of the Bali Hyatt Hotel, Mr Melvin Labra, Mr Setapong Lekawatana, Mrs Gretchen Liu, Mr Leonard Lueras, Mr Islay Lyons, Dr and Mrs Thomas Macmillan, Mr Leland Miyano, Mrs May Moir, Mr Frank Morgan, Ms Linda Moriarity, Mrs Fern Pietsch, M.R. Kukrit Pramoj, Dr Yoneo Sagawa of the Lyon Arboretum, Khunying Lurasakdi Sampatisiri, Mr Victor Sassoon, Mr George Staples, Mr Jurg Suter, Mr Hiroshi Tagami, Mrs Jean Thomas, Mrs Bonnie Tinsley of the Singapore Botanical Gardens, Mrs Anne Tofield, Mr Chaiwut Tulyadhan, Mr Richard Via, Ms Marisa Viravaidhya, Mr and Mrs Yvan Van Outrive, Mr Prasart Vongsakul, Mr William Waterfall, Mr Lyndon Wester, Mr Made Wijaya (Michael White) of Pacific Landscape Design, Mr and Mrs Wiya Wawo-Runtu, Dr Keith Wooliams of the Waimea Arboretum, Ms Ploenpit Wuttayagon.

223

THE TROPICAL GARDEN

THE TROPICAL GARDEN

with 365 full-color illustrations

Text by William Warren

Photographs by Luca Invernizzi Tettoni